The Humanism of Italy, which treats of the changes and innovations that marked the period of the Renaissance, reflects the author's emphasis on history as a slow process in which the present can be understood only as a continuation of the past. One of the first American historians to challenge the prevailing conception of the Renaissance as marking an abrupt change, Henry Osborn Taylor traces the roots of humanism to the so-called Dark Ages and shows that the emancipation of the intellect had begun then.

Taylor belongs to the generation of outstanding American historians that includes Lynn Thorndike, James Harvey Robinson, and Preserved Smith. He was born in New York City on December 5, 1856, and died there on April 13, 1941. Taylor was graduated from Harvard in 1878 and received a degree in law from Columbia University in 1881. However, law was not his calling, and he soon began to devote himself to the study of Western culture. He lectured at various universities, and in 1927 he served as president of the American Historical Association.

In addition to *Thought and Expression in the Sixteenth Century,* Taylor's works include *Ancient Ideals, A Study of the Intellectual and Spiritual Growth from Early Times to the Establishment of Christianity* (2 vols., 2nd ed. 1913), *Freedom of the Mind in History* (2nd ed. 1924), and *A Historian's Creed* (1939). His most important work is *The Medieval Mind* (2 vols., 5th ed. 1938).

The five books of *Thought and Expression in the Sixteenth Century,* all available in Collier paperbacks, are:

The Humanism of Italy (AS 437)

Erasmus and Luther (AS 438)

The French Mind (AS 439)

The English Mind (AS 440)

Philosophy and Science in the Sixteenth Century (AS 441)

HENRY OSBORN TAYLOR

THE

OF

HUMANISM
ITALY

BOOK I OF *Thought and Expression in the Sixteenth Century*

Sixteenth Century

COLLIER BOOKS
NEW YORK, N.Y.

This Collier Books edition is published by arrangement with The President and Fellows of Harvard College.

Collier Books is a division of The Crowell-Collier Publishing Company.

First Collier Books Edition 1962

About the Author

HENRY OSBORN TAYLOR belongs to the outstanding generation of American historians that includes Lynn Thorndike, James Harvey Robinson, and Preserved Smith. He was born December 5, 1856, in New York City, and died there on April 13, 1941. Taylor was graduated from Harvard in 1878 and received a degree in law from Columbia University in 1881. Law was not his calling, however, and he soon began to devote himself to the study of Western culture.

Thought and Expression in the Sixteenth Century (2 vols., 1920) and *The Mediaeval Mind* (2 vols., 5th ed. 1938) are classics in the historiography of ideas in America.

Other books by Taylor include his first work, *Ancient Ideals, a Study of the Intellectual and Spiritual Growth from Early Times to the Establishment of Christianity* (2 vols., 2nd ed. 1913), *Freedom of the Mind in History* (2nd ed. 1924), and *A Historian's Creed* (1939).

Thought and Expression in the Sixteenth Century is now published by Collier Books in five volumes, each of which may be read independently: *The Humanism of Italy, Erasmus and Luther, The French Mind, The English Mind,* and *Philosophy and Science in the Renaissance* are the titles of the separate volumes in this new edition.

Note

Since 1860, when Burckhardt published his *Civilization of the Renaissance in Italy,* a formidable amount of scholarship, much of it passionate, has been expended in an attempt to extend and correct Burckhardt's conception of the Renaissance. In the process, our sense of the function of the Renaissance in our culture has undergone profound change. The effects of this change are not difficult to perceive: the kinds of problems with which the Renaissance was concerned—religious, cultural, political, educational—are not only similar to our own, but in addition, reveal a definite historical continuity with the problems confronting us today.

The perceptive analysis of this continuity is the first merit of Henry Osborn Taylor's *Thought and Expression in the Sixteenth Century,* one of the first comprehensive surveys of the Renaissance to appear since Burckhardt's work. *The Humanism of Italy,* the first volume of *Thought and Expression,* is a selective and balanced exploration of the lives and personalities of those who raised problems and issues still relevant to us.

No doubt *The Humanism of Italy* is open to correction of detail and interpretation; but no general survey has taken the place of its sharp mapping out of the literature, the art, the politics, and the history by which the Italian genius provided Europe with a new age.

Contents

Preface

MY PURPOSE IS TO GIVE an intellectual survey of the sixteenth century. I would set forth the human susceptibilities and faculties of this alluring time, its tastes, opinions and appreciations, as they expressed themselves in scholarship and literature, in philosophy and science, and in religious reform. Italian painting is presented briefly as the supreme self-expression of the Italians.

The more typical intellectual interests of the fifteenth century also are discussed for their own sake, while those of the previous time are treated as introductory. I have tried to show the vital continuity between the prior mediaeval development and the period before us.

The mind must fetch a far compass if it would see the sixteenth century truly. Every stage in the life and thought of Europe represents a passing phase, which is endowed with faculties not begotten of itself, and brings forth much that is not exclusively its own. For good or ill, for patent progress, or apparent retrogression, its capacities, idiosyncrasies and productions belong, in large measure, to the whole, which is made up of past as well as present, the latter pregnant with the future. Yet, though fed upon the elements (sometimes the refuse) of the past, each time seems to develop according to its own nature. Waywardly, foolishly, or with wholesome originality, it evolves a novel temperament and novel thoughts.

We shall treat the fifteenth and sixteenth centuries as a final and objective present; and all that went before will be regarded as a past which entered into them. It included pagan Antiquity, Judaism and the Gospel, the influence of the fecund East, the contribution of the Christian Fathers,

11

—this whole store of knowledge and emotion, not merely as it came into being, but in its changing progress through the Middle Ages, until it entered the thought of our period and became the stimulus or suggestion of its feeling. Distinctive mediaeval creations likewise must be included, seeing that they also entered formatively into the constitutions of later men. The Middle Ages helped antiquity to shape the faculties and furnish the tastes of the sixteenth century. These faculties and tastes were then applied to what the past seemed also to offer as from a distinct and separate platform. Only by realizing the action of these formative and contributive agencies, shall we perceive this period's true relationships, and appreciate its caused and causal being, begotten of the past, yet vital (as each period is) with its own spirit, and big with a modernity which was not yet.

Two pasts may be distinguished, the one remote, the other proximate. The former may be taken as consisting of the antique world as it became its greater self, and then as it crumbled, while its thought and mood were assuming those forms in which they passed into the Middle Ages. The proximate or immediate past was the mediaeval time, itself progressing century after century under the influence of whatever had entered into it, chiefly through those last solvent and transition centuries in which the remote past ended.

The Middle Ages and the fifteenth or sixteenth century bore the same fundamental relationship to this remote past. Each succeeding mediaeval century, besides inheriting what had become known in the time directly preceding it, endeavored to reach back to the remote past for further treasure. Thus the twelfth century sought to reach behind the eleventh, in order to learn more of the greater past, and the thirteenth reached behind the twelfth. So Petrarch, in the fourteenth, would reach behind the vociferously damned thirteenth century to antiquity itself; and the fifteenth century humanists endeavored to do likewise. That century, like Petrarch's time, drew from its immediate mediaeval past as copiously as each mediaeval century drew from its predecessor, and *willy nilly* resembled the mediaeval centuries in striving to reach back of them for treasures previously undisclosed.

One thinks of the transmitted influence of the past, whether remote or proximate, as knowledge and suggestion, as intellectual or emotional or social material to be appropriated and made further use of. It is well to think of it also as flowing on in modes of expression, which constitute the finished form of the matter, whether the form lie in language or in the figures of plastic art. Thoughts and emotions cannot pass from one time to another save in modes of their expression. And the more finished and perfect, the more taking, the more beautiful, the form of expression, the more enduring will be its influence and effect. The seemingly formless material which is transmitted orally or in manuscripts or printed books from age to age, had necessarily reached some mode of expression, however vile. And although much wretched matter has come down through time, we may not ascribe its survival to the shortcomings of its form, but rather to the fact that somehow in its wretchedness and intellectual squalor it suited the squalid ignorance of men.

So it is fruitful to think, for instance, of each mediaeval century, as well as of the great sixteenth, as drawing the language of its thinking from the past, and then building up its own forms of thinking and expression. Each province of discipline furnishes concepts and a vocabulary. As each century appropriates them and makes them its own, they become its modes of thought, and the forms of its self-expression. Thus not only thought, but the language of expression, is handed on with enhancements from generation to generation. Each generation uses the thought, and expresses itself in the forms and concepts, which it has made its own—has made into its self-expression. Yet there is some change, some increase, some advance. To the transformation of inherited thought and phrase into modes of self-expression, each century or generation brings a tone and temper of its own, perhaps some change of attitude toward life, and at all events the increment and teaching of the experience which has come to it through living.

Difficulties of arrangement confront a work like the present. Shall it cleave to racehood and nationality or follow topics? Topics ignore racial lines and geographical boundaries.

The plan must bend to the demands on it. Sometimes racial traits dominate an individual, and the conditions of his life and land shape his career, even a great career like Luther's. A national situation may point the substance of an issue, as, in England, in Wyclif's controversy with the papacy. For quite another illustration, one may observe how a diversity of interest and taste between Italians and Frenchmen impressed a different purpose and manner upon classical studies in Italy and France.

On the other hand such a story as that of the advance of the physical sciences in the fifteenth and sixteenth centuries has little to do with land or race; the votaries belong to every people, and pursue their investigations indifferently in their own countries or where foreign localities offer greater advantages. So a general survey should follow the course of the most dominant and vital elements.

A kindred question goes to the roots of the truth of phenomena: should one adhere to a temporal arrangement, century by century, or follow sequences of influence and effect across the imaginary boundaries of these arbitrary time divisions? While it is convenient to speak of "centuries," one is always pursuing the vital continuity of effect. The virtue of fruitful effort passes into future achievement. One seeks to follow facts in their progeny. Yet this is difficult, since the genealogical tree is infinitely ramified, and every event, every achievement, has as many forbears as a human being! The truthfulness of events lies in the process of *becoming,* rather than in the concrete phenomenon which catches our attention. It would be as foolish to end the consideration of Petrarch with his death as it would be to treat him as if he and his work and influence really began the day when he was born, or first read Cicero.

Nothing begins or ends. We may even think of all that is, or ever was or will be, as one mighty self-evolving present, which holds the effective being, the becoming, of the past, and contains the future, of which this present is in turn the becoming.

HENRY OSBORN TAYLOR

New York, May, 1920.

The Humanism of Italy

Chapter 1

The Litterae Humaniores:
Petrarch and Boccaccio

HUMANISM IN A LITERARY SENSE is usually thought of as
referring to humane studies, the *litterae humaniores*. Their
academic field has always been the literature and plastic
arts of Greece and Rome. The conception seems just, as
far as it reaches. For, in the main, the thought, the literature and the plastic arts of Greece and Rome are the record
and expression of man living on the earth, and all things
are conceived, reflected on, and felt in their relationships
to humanity. Occasionally Greek thought and its expression soared beyond the sphere of man, as sometimes with
Plato and his spiritual descendants. And the world of
nature was embraced by Aristotle and those who preceded
or followed him in physical researches. Among the Greeks
there were wise physicians, great physicists, mathemati-
cians and astronomers. Greek achievements in physical
science are liable to be ignored because we have gone so
far beyond them.

But in the sixteenth century, Greece still offered much
physical science for profitable study by the learned world,
which was only beginning a systematic investigation of the
phenomena of nature. Interest in natural phenomena was
as yet scarcely de-humanized, or accepted and pursued
without regard to the assumed connection between the
world of nature and the fortunes or designs of men. Nature bristled with portents. The science of Astrology observed the heavens for horoscopes and looked to celestial

19

influences upon men. But Astronomy was Astrology de-humanized and set upon the basis of its own explanatory truth regarding the movements of the sun and moon and stars.

Such astronomy had been pursued by the astronomers of Alexandria, who still did not neglect its astrological bearings. With the Greeks, natural science generally was mindful of the connection between the apparent ends of nature and the welfare or miscarriages of men. Greek science was apt to be anthropomorphic, and Greek philosophy in its treatment of physical and metaphysical truth remained genially human. In all Greek thinking, man remained the πόλις, the city-state, whence thoughts as citizens went forth to return with sheaves of knowledge that were to be transformed to human wisdom.

So philosophy and natural science, as part of the Greek consideration of life, are not excluded from Greek humanism, which brought all intellectual interests into its web and kept them circling around man. This is why, although we no longer quite determine our thinking by what Plato said or Aristotle, we cherish their metaphysics as a beautiful and still moving human creation, closely knit into the intellectual needs of man. And the Greek and Latin literature, the poetry, the immortal stories of human fortunes, the profound and inclusive consideration of human life, all these have never ceased to charm the generations of men, nor have they ceased to be perennial fonts of human illumination and consideration of human life. They are a well which no one can exhaust, but from which every one may draw according to the capacities of his understanding.

Accordingly the literature of Rome and Greece, the Classics *par excellence,* have been called the humanities; the reading and study of them have been called humane studies, and their votaries have been known as humanists. Yet the proper humanist, whether belonging to the sixteenth century or to other times, is such not only in his pursuits, but in his mind. He must be as that which he reads and loves, interested and absorbed in man here on this earth, in his individuality and accordant or disaccordant fortunes, in his loves and hates, his fancies and desires, in all that makes the atmosphere of mortal life.

He will be not merely a reader of the classics, but an individual of definite temperament and taste, with which his favorite studies accord. His pursuits are the fruit of his desires and opinions, the fruit of his personality in fine. Consequently his humanism with its occupations, preoccupations, and achievement, is an expression of himself. And when there are many humanists, living and reading and studying at the same time, delighting in the discussion and exploitation of their common pursuits, humanism becomes a phase of the time, a phase of its self-expression. Such humanism is not apt to flourish now, because our horizons are too large, and we have a different consciousness of a universe, in which man is a rather recent counter and one that possibly may also pass, as the creatures of prior geologic ages have had their aeons and have passed away. It is not that we constantly look beyond to another and immortal sphere, as most people did in the Middle Ages, and many humanists in the next centuries more perfunctorily. But natural science, physical science, biological science, all for their own sake, have their innings now, and the man-centered equilibrium of the old humanists is at least tipped, if not upset.

In the fifteenth and sixteenth centuries a large proportion of active-minded men devoted themselves to humane studies, possessed humanistic tempers, and took a humanistic view of life. They were absorbed in the mortal life of man, their own especially; in its conduct, deeds and passions, in its whims and desires and fancies, in its success or failures, and in the moral, philosophical, esthetic consideration of it all. They read and studied the great writings which were the universal and glorious exponents of these fascinating matters, and they were drawn by everything connected with that antique world of which these classic writers were the flower. So humanism may be deemed a phase of the self-expression of the fifteenth and sixteenth centuries and a characteristic feature of their entire mental progress.

I

The disparate humanity of the early Middle Ages required some centuries to develop a full complement of humane qualities. Only the antique Latin literature could be the guide, and furnish the means, of such development. Too constantly this literature of *litterae humaniores* was used wrongly and wilfully as the vehicle of what it did not contain. Men found in it instruction, set in allegory, touching the mysteries of all the worlds and man their denizen. Yet no century was completely lacking in humanists, who, perhaps in a hampered or uninstructed way, looked at the classics truly, and found in them solace and suggestion touching life.

The *litterae humaniores* were admirably cultivated by certain men in the twelfth century; [1] yet as it closed, the absorbing interest in Aristotelian scholasticism began to prove detrimental to letters, although it did not hamper the splendid advance in building and sculpture and glass painting, which is as great a glory of the thirteenth century as Thomas Aquinas himself. The main inspiration of that Gothic art was religious, even theological, rather than humane. Yet it embraced and seemed to carry heavenward humanity's daily round of tasks and interests, thus representing an ennobled or sublimated humanism. But while it lifted human nature, it did less to enlarge it or promote the capacity for mortal happiness and joy.

This was to be the office of the Latin and Greek Classics. Through the Middle Ages and afterwards, they were to expand and equip humanity upon the earth, and uplift it so far as might be without drawing it up to heaven. They were to enrich human life by humanizing all that made man's environment, transforming the world in which he found himself into objects of human perception, interest, sentiment. They also furnished their lovers with a

[1] Cf. Taylor, *The Mediaeval Mind,* Chap. XXXI. My references to this work are to the paging and chapters of the second and third editions.

variety of just reflections upon life, and fostered in them the habit of consideration.

The vigorous literary use of the vernaculars had, by the fourteenth century, lowered the vitality and impaired the clarity of the Latin still employed by educated men. Especially, the Latin of scholastic philosophy and political controversy had become a dreadful example of how a language could be mishandled. While the learned of no one country held the monopoly of this abuse, still the obnoxious jargon of scholasticism was in the main a product of northern lands, where interest in theology had possessed so many minds. Men who were free from that obsession would naturally detest its lingo. But in distorting the Latin tongue, the treatises upon the civil law were not so far behind, and it happened that the strongest personal reaction against these logical and linguistic decadences arose in one who hated scholasticism and had no liking for the law, to which his father would have apprenticed him. This reaction proved a lasting irritant with Petrarch, although it was not a dominant influence in his life.

For such, one turns to his admiration for antiquity and his love of the classic Latin literature. Thousands of his countrymen had felt the like before him. One thinks not only of Dante himself, but of the Paduan Mussato, who cared for Latin letters and was crowned poet in Padua in 1314.[2] In Italy the cult of antiquity, with a dumb cultivation of the classics, had not been as sporadic, or as pressed upon by other intellectual interests, as in the north. It was always there, in more or less clear consciousness, working with more or less energy. In the fourteenth century it was natural that a love of classic letters should spring up in an Italian breast; and there were men in Italy ready to catch the fire—just as in England, when Wyclif's ideas were once started, there were men of kindred mind to carry them on.

But Petrarch was a great inaugurator. While young,

---

[2] Cf. Zardo, *Mussato*, (Padua 1884). He was particularly studious of Livy, Seneca and Ovid.

he was recognized as *poeta,* a title dear to Italian ears and hearts. That gave him popular acclaim. He possessed a penetrating and sensitive intelligence. He had also a quality helpful to a successful man of letters, the faculty of pose,—in his case the faculty of posing for what he really was, with added pretensions to much that he was not. He never laid aside the pose of gifted poet, supreme man of letters: restorer of the glories of antiquity. If this was pose, it was also fact. But such a poet, scholar, restorer of a greater past, should be above personal vanities, free from envy, superior to greed. Petrarch posed as such a one, in his writings and before his world; and such he was not. For he was vain and envious, and if not inordinately greedy, he was not the *divitiarum contemptor eximius* [3] that he calls himself in his *Letter to Posterity;* in which he otherwise elaborates his pose: "In others I perceived pride. not in myself, *et cum parvus fuerim, semper minor judicio meo fui.* [4] Kings and princes cherished me, I know not why, and I was with some of them as if they rather were with me!" Even in writings devoted to searchings of himself, but which also safeguarded his pose, one sees that he was enormously self-satisfied.

If these traits give a certain smugness to his character, they helped to make him, in his lifetime and with posterity, the most successful of literary men: successful in leading his life as he wished and in accomplishing what he was capable of; successful in impressing himself upon contemporaries and posterity exactly as he would be taken. Although he thought himself unfortunate in the hour of his birth, he was most fortunate both in the hour and place. For his genius led him to those very pursuits to which Italy, and after her the north, were soon to turn with unprecedented ardor. While he lived, large and distinguished circles of like-minded admirers revered him as unique in his knowledge and virtuosity. It became an amiable con-

---

[3] "a preeminent despiser of wealth."
[4] "and since I was but an insignificant man, I was always smaller in stature than my own estimate of myself."

vention among them to speak of him as equalling Cicero in eloquence and Virgil in poetry. Boccaccio says it, and Nelli writing thus: Te solum legens, Maronem Ciceronemque legam.[5] The same sweetly friendly Nelli begs to be numbered among his little slaves (servulos), and accounts himself happy to have lived in the same age with him. He describes the excitement over the supposed, and then assured, arrival of a letter from Petrarch: pulsat nuntius januam—a cry bursts forth, the servants run to usher in the bearer, who delivers to us "thy letters, nay rather, thy most precious pearls." [6] Who would have written this to Dante or Michelangelo? Or when did the great of this earth come to watch Dante composing his *Inferno,* as Pandolfo Malatesta, although sick, is brought supported by his servants to see Petrarch in his own chair, surrounded by his books? Petrarch was an excellent flatterer himself, especially of Kings from whom he sought emolument and honor. His praise of the epigrams of Robert, King of Naples, deserved much.[7]

In fine, before his death his fame was spread abroad, and afterwards grew mightier, because he had been in life a lovely poet in the *volgare,* and above that had been the lofty leader and achiever in what was becoming a dominating intellectual movement. He was thus the prototypal embodiment of the rising zeal for classical study, and of the best critical phases of it, for he saw the classics as clearly as any one with his available lights could see. He embodied also the ambition and misdirected effort of the coming period, in Italy at least, to compose works in Latin prose and metre, modelled upon classical standards of beauty. His attitude toward his own exquisite poems in the *volgare* was that which was held to be correct by later Italian humanists, who often professed to despise the vulgar tongue, including their own indiscretions in the same.

5 *Lettres de Francesco Nelli à Pétrarque,* ed. H. Cochin (Champion 1892), Ep. 14—Boccaccio in *Ep. Seniles,* XVII, 2.

6 Ep. 11. *Lettres de Francesco Nelli à Pétrarque.*

7 Sen. I, 6; Fam. IV, 3. Petrarch's letters—Familiares, Variae, Seniles—are usually thus cited: Fam., Var., Sen.

Finally there was nothing in his career or character that the coming time could not admire. He had professed his contempt for wealth, and declared his freedom from such little weaknesses as envy and malice; and even if he were not quite taken at his word (like statements were to be humanist conventions), his foibles could not appear as blots to later men whose characters openly presented the same. For most of them were vain, self-conscious and affected, and addicted to envy, hatred, and malice and all unseemliness.

As touching Petrarch, we may say, for ourselves, that like Cicero, whom he adored, and like Erasmus after him, he was a great man of letters, and, like them, a man one must sympathize with in order to judge rightly, and "be to his faults a little blind." *"Libris satiari nequeo,"* [8] he writes in a pleasant letter on books and reading (Fam. III, 17). Wherever there are books, some men are born with a sheer love of them, and it may be with that added impulse toward expression which makes a man of letters. In the fourteenth century what should a scholarly Italian read, when he disliked the law and detested scholasticism? —what indeed, except the Latin classics, especially when he was a poet, and born with a love of literary form? Despising his own age, foolishly wishing to have lived in some other time, he attached himself to the cult of antiquity: "Incubui unice inter multa ad notitiam vetustatis," he says in his *Letter to Posterity.* But he is glad to have been born in Italy and not in the Scythian north. He praises Roman Italy in comparison with Greece, and the Latin as compared with the Greek literature, of which he knew nothing save from report.

Naturally when Petrarch came to Rome, he felt a great sensation—how many pilgrim hearts had swelled at the sight of those towers, through all the Middle Ages! It was there that his heart's vainest wish was to be fulfilled, when he was given the laurel crown upon the Capitol. He was

8 "I cannot indulge myself enough in books."

acquainted with that self-deceived arouser of enthusiasms, Rienzi—Tribune of the Roman People!—and writes to him in words as foolish as the shouts of the Roman populace: "Salve, noster Camille, noster Romule," (or by whatever name thou wouldst be called)—"salve Romanae libertatis, Romanae pacis, Romanae tranquillitatis auctor!" [9] (Var. 48.)

Toward the Catholic faith Petrarch stood as a mediaeval man, but with some supervening waverings which, in our eyes, make his religious attitude more reasonable. He had read the Fathers, especially Augustine, whose *Confessions* he liked to have at hand; he took them with him in that ascent of Mt. Ventoux, which was suggested to him by reading in Livy how the King of Macedon ascended Mt. Haemas in Thrace, from which both the Euxine and the Adriatic could be seen (Fam. IV, 1). Petrarch, a poor climber, used the difficulties of the ascent to illustrate how hard is virtue to attain—the Middle Ages had always put mountains to this symbolic moral use! At the top Petrarch's thoughts run in the old channels of sin and concupiscence as he reads Augustine's *Confessions*. An odd place to worry over concupiscence and read Augustine!

Like any scholar, Petrarch was fond of quiet and solitude. Replying sympathetically (Fam. IX, 14) to an ecclesiastic's letter praising the solitary life, and speaking for himself, he declares it practically impossible to live or die well save in solitude—"natura dux nostra nos solitarios fecit." And he is capable of decrying carnal love and approving of monastic asceticism. (Fam. X, 3 and 5.) Yet it is easy to see that his reason for preferring the solitary life is the scholar's reason simply, just as he points out in his *De Vita Solitaria,* that the *occupatus* living in the world is exposed to more interruptions and annoyances than the

[9] "Hail to thee, our Camillus, hail to thee, our Romulus. Hail to thee, author of Roman peace, Roman liberty, and Roman serenity."

solitarius. The imaginary dialogue with Augustine, which Petrarch named *Secretum Meum,*[10] seems to discuss how man may win his best tranquillity. Augustine searches into Petrarch's faults, reproves them gently, recognizes his freedom at least from the sin of envy, points out the incompatibility of carnal passion with man's best peace of mind, and shows the remedy in clarity of judgment, unity of aim, and strength of will to follow it. Petrarch sees the vanity of striving after many things, and has qualms as to the classic studies to which he is addicted—so had St. Jerome and many a mediaeval lover of the classics!

Petrarch had solved the last difficult problem by leading the life of a man of letters. In this he had found his happiness and peace. And with the practical wisdom with which he had conducted his own life, he writes to his friend Boccaccio when both were grey. The latter, seized with compunctions, was proposing to abandon secular themes and studies, and prepare for death somewhat more exclusively than he had done. Petrarch views the situation fairly: an old scholar surely should not discard the studies which have been the occupation of his life, and are the best solace for old age. Without such needless sacrifice, he can still prepare for death (Sen. I, 5).

So Petrarch's attitude toward religion was that of the man of scholarly tastes, not deeply religious, who decorously recognized, and occasionally felt, religion's claims. Somewhat more firmly than a man of like temperament would have done a century before, he kept religion in its proper place. He would not have men think him either a Ciceronian or a Platonist, but of a surety a Christian. He was, however, always ready to attack the current scholasticism, though, of course, as a man of antique letters, he must be himself a follower of philosophy. "I love philosophy," he says, "not the loquacious, scholastic, windy brand . . . but the true, which lives in souls rather than in books." (Fam. XII, 3.) One suspects that he did not know much

10 Translated by W. H. Draper. *Petrarch's Secret,* &c. (London, 1911.)

about what he was condemning or what he was praising. He took from Cicero or Augustine the idea of Plato's primacy, and in his *De Ignorantia* [11] conducts a moderate literary polemic against Aristotle. Yet he professed to respect that master, while he despised his hair-splitting so-called followers. *"Vir ardentis ingenii,"* [12] he once called him. Nevertheless, much as he knew or did not know about it, Petrarch's acute intelligence perceived the emptiness of the current scholasticism. It was also characteristic of him that he should take a rational view of dreams (Fam. V, 7), see the falsity of astrology (Sen. III, 1) and note the quackery in the medicine then practiced. Nor would he accept Virgil as a magician, although Boccaccio was inclined to.[13]

As a scholar, Petrarch has rightly remained illustrious. He was not such incidentally, or in the midst of other occupations; but primarily and unremittingly with his whole bent of mind and purpose. Of course, he was an ardent assembler of manuscripts, the tools and means of his vocation. He passionately desired to collect and own them, and have the best and most correct. He was, perhaps had to be, a bibliophile as well as a scholar, the leader of that multitude of ardent lovers of the classics who loved to collect manuscripts, and had to be collectors in order to be students. Of course, one must not think of this as a new phenomenon in the world, although it was to manifest itself on an unprecedented scale. Through all the mediaeval centuries, scholars had been collectors of their precious books. "I am eagerly collecting a library; and as formerly at Rome and elsewhere in Italy, so likewise in Germany and Belgium, I have obtained copyists and manuscripts with a mass of money, and the help of friends in those parts. Permit me to beg of you also to promote this

---

[11] Ed. Capelli (Champion, Paris, 1906).
[12] "A man of fiery genius."
[13] De Nolhac, *Pétrarque et l'humanisme*, pp. 126-7 (Paris, Champion, 1907).

end. We will append at the end of this letter a list of those writers we wish copied." This extract is not from one of Petrarch's letters, though he wrote many like it; but from a letter of Gerbert who became Pope Sylvester II in the year 999.[14]

But undoubtedly Petrarch marks a new stage in the study and appreciation of the classics. And naturally. In a general way, if allowance be made for definite interruptions and catastrophes, and different fields of interest and effort, each mediaeval century shows an intellectual advance. Accordingly, a revival of classical study in the fourteenth century would start from a base of maturer intelligence than in the twelfth. On the other hand, being but the great pioneer of the movement, Petrarch's knowledge was less than that of the following generations of humanists who were stimulated and assisted by his labors. The chief gap in his knowledge was his ignorance of Greek, which made his perspective faulty and left his ordering of classical authors still mediaeval. Says he with comical sententiousness: "Plato magnus vir, magnus Pythagoras, magnus Aristoteles, magnus Varro" (Fam. XVII, 1). The last had been a great figure in the Middle Ages.

Within the range of its knowledge, his acute mind discriminated justly. His idol in prose was Cicero; through long study and devotion he seemed to himself to have attained a personal intimacy with him. Yet, as it was only in middle life that he found a manuscript of Cicero's letters, he did not form his own epistolary style on them. In fact, Seneca influenced him as much as Cicero. One may remark that not only in the Middle Ages, but from Petrarch's time onward through the fifteenth and sixteenth centuries, humanists took kindly to the Latin writers of the silver and even the brass age, and when they came to know Greek, they preferred the later Greek authors. Some reasons for this are clear. Both the late Latin and late Greek writers were more cosmopolitan and easier to appreciate

14 Ep. 44, Havet's Edition. Gerbert was not single in these tastes—see *The Mediaeval Mind,* chaps. XII and XIII.

than their greater and often austere predecessors. The Romans themselves had not cared for Aeschylus and Aristophanes, who, like Plato, were distinguished by a sublime provincialism. More promiscuous and readily tangible human affinities were offered by the Hellenistic Plutarch. For analogous reasons, Seneca was the really popular moralist, and continued so through the fifteenth and sixteenth centuries. He was closer to the Christian mood, and at so many points touched the commonplace nature of man. Thus we may also see why Petrarch sought moral instruction from Ovid's *Elegies,* while he revered and imitated Virgil.

Following the examples of scholars before him, whether living in the fifth century or the thirteenth, Petrarch took the classic poets allegorically. One of his later letters (Sen. IV, 5) has much to say of the moral or allegorical interpretation of Virgil, and maintains that the end and subject —finis et subjectum—of the *Aeneid* is the perfect man, or man made perfect—*vir perfectus.* To discover an allegory in a narrative means commonly to moralize the narrative, generalize it from a moral point of view, or generalize a lesson from it. Allegory is a kind of generalization. And sometimes, as we follow an allegorical interpretation of a story, for example Petrarch's interpretation of the *Aeneid,* we perceive that much of it is but a pointing of its "lesson." Some such lesson, or revelation of the universal in the concrete, lies in every great story. And who shall say that the poet did not feel or mean it too, at least when he is so thoughtful, even contemplative, a writer as Virgil? Is it not possible also that the Greek critics, who held before Virgil's day that all great poetry should be taken allegorically—is it not possible that sometimes they may have meant little more than when we say such and such a narration carries a lesson?

The trouble was that some of those critics and interpreters overelaborated and specialized their allegorical interpretation, making it quite beside the probable intention of the author, pointing it, as in the case of the Old Testament, to apologetic uses, or making it silly and un-

likely, as in the case of a great poem like the *Aeneid*.[15]
Thus while Petrarch, in his letters just referred to, sometimes says little more than we ourselves might choose to
fancy as the "lesson" of the tale, he is also, like his mediaeval forbears, or the grammarians of the transition centuries, quite capable of foolishness. The Virgilian picture
(*Aen.* IV, 554) of Aeneas, when all was ready to set sail
from Carthage, asleep on his ship, *celsa in puppi,* he inter-
prets as *alta in mente certo proposito conquiescens*—or,
so to speak, at peace in his high purpose. We do not think
that Virgil meant this by *celsa in puppi.*

So for Petrarch all great poetry carries allegory. He in-
tends his own Latin poetry to be taken in the same way.
He sends his eclogue *Parthenias* to his brother, expound-
ing it allegorically (Fam. X, 4). In fact, it is difficult to
understand his eclogues without a key to the symbolism of
their language; in one of them, the *Bucolicum Carmen,*
in the person of Silvius, he explains to his brother through
allegories his need to write the *Africa*.[16] What shall one
say of that supreme effort of Petrarch after immortal
fame? Few human beings have read it! [17] It seems to open
with heavy notes of egotism and adulation; there is no epic
plunge *in medias res!* As one proceeds, one finds classic
involutions without the classic movement. It seems to go
through the motions of the *Aeneid* stylistically; yet does
not move. With its borrowed thoughts and borrowed
phrases, not reproduced *in ipsissimis verbis,* it affects one
as a sort of pseudocopy.

One gathers from it the way in which Petrarch sought
to form his style. He advises not to copy the words, but
rather to master the classic thoughts. He would not slavishly imitate the phrasing of one writer, but avail of the
excellences of many: nec huius stilum aut illius, sed unum
nostrum conflatum ex pluribus habeamus. Not everyone

---

[15] See *The Mediaeval Mind,* Chap. XXXI. (Vol. II, p. 141-2.)
[16] *Poemata minora Francisci Petrarcae,* ed. Rosetti, (Milan
1823); *Il Bucolicum Carmen,* ed. Avila (Padua 1906).
[17] The present writer has only read *at* it.

can learn to write well by reading the classics; he must have, or gain through them, a serene and well equipped mind: he must be something, or have become something, in himself: "For speech is no slight index of the mind, nor the mind a slight director of speech; one depends on the other." [18]

Many a scholar in the generations and centuries before Petrarch had tried to write as well as possible, had striven for style and form. The vernacular poetry of the troubadours of Provence was mainly a thing of form; and often a mediaeval Latin writer in the twelfth or thirteenth century modelled his style quite consciously on the classics or on the approved writers of his time. With Petrarch, the effort for style has become portentously self-conscious. He is the forerunner of those generations of Italian humanists who pursued "art for art's sake," and by striving utterly for form in writing, emptied themselves of substance. This forerunner, who himself was not always creative, tried so consciously for form, that most of his works have entered the company of those which are not read, but read about. His letters, carefully edited by him, are interesting as a record of his life. They may have done much to bring into vogue the *genre* of epistolary writing consisting of intimate short self-revealing letters or essays upon topics other than theology and politics. Beyond them, and perhaps his *Secretum,* who but a special student reads Petrarch's Latin works? In some of them the dullness of the Middle Ages seems clothed upon, as in the *De remediis utriusque fortunae,* where every conceivable good, and then every conceivable ill of human life is presented *seriatim,* with opposed or compensating considerations.

The *De viris illustribus,* [19] a work of greater rhetorical effort, is more alive by reason of its subject, the life histories of Roman worthies. Its substance was drawn from Livy, where that was possible, or again from Caesar's

---

[18] Fam. I, 7 & 8; XXIII, 19. See his later remarks on style in a letter to Bruni. Sen. II, 3.

[19] Ed. Razzolini (Bologna 1874).

Commentaries, which Petrarch, in common with men before and also after him, ascribed to one Julius Celsus. Petrarch's principle of selection, as given in his preface, is to use only those matters which illustrate the virtues or their contraries; for the *fructuosus finis* of historians is to present that which the reader ought either to follow or avoid:—which is a way of writing history for the purpose of moral improvement, as more than one mediaeval compiler had done. The preface turns also to posterity, and expresses the author's wish to be dear to it. As the work warms up to the important people, it becomes good rhetorical exposition. Such is the story of Camillus; and a long, intelligently composed biography of Caesar is presented.

It is illuminating to compare Petrarch with Hildebert of Lavardin and John of Salisbury, noteworthy humanists of the eleventh and twelfth centuries.[20] The former, who lived from about 1055 to 1130, ended his life as Archbishop of Tours. He was an enthusiastic lover of the classic Latin literature, and the spell of the antique lay on him. Visiting Rome, he wrote admirable elegies upon its ruined state, elegies in which the gods are made to marvel at the beauty of their own sculptured images. The prose of his letters was not disturbed by attempts at a pseudo-classic style; it has grace as well as force. His letters were studied as models after his death. John of Salisbury was born about 1115 and died as Bishop of Chartres in 1180. He was the friend both of Becket and of Henry II, and in his time had sat at the feet of many famous teachers, Abelard for instance, as well as Bernard of Chartres. He gives a charming picture of the latter's method of teaching. Always an advocate of a thorough classical education, John poured his sarcasms on those who "preferred to seem rather than be, philosophers and professors of the arts, engaging to impart the whole of philosophy in less than three years, or even two." He was quite at home with the

[20] See chapters XXXI and XXXII of *The Mediaeval Mind,* and Vol. II, pp. 403 sqq.

classic authors, citing their lives as readily and as appositely as he cited Scripture. A student and clever historian of the antique philosophy, he knew as much of it as was possible for a man living before the unearthing of Aristotle. His writings as well as his personality were imbued with its spirit; he applied its teachings in his life and contemplation, and could look with even eye on all things. *Moderatrix omnium* was his favorite term for philosophy.

According to the present writer's taste, these men wrote Latin more agreeably than Petrach. Since they were active in affairs of Church and State, they did not, like him, follow letters exclusively. Their writings do not disclose such absorbing curiosity as to everything connected with antiquity. It would indeed be hard to find anyone before Petrarch so completely devoted as himself to the study of the classics and so consciously striving to be intimate with antiquity. Moreover, while these men had a just and true feeling for the classics, they lived when men knew less and had experienced less. One cannot expect to find them as mature as he. The clearest difference between them lay in their intellectual environment and in the immediate destinies of their respective epochs, with reference to the *litterae humaniores* of Rome and Greece. The twelfth century was the best period of mediaeval Latin writing, and also one when many scholars cared for the classics and read them diligently. But even then there were men of other minds, who looked on Latin letters merely as a means towards quite different pursuits. Before many decades, the dominant intellectual interests of the time moved away from the *litterae humaniores* somewhat more definitely. The period of the great and, on the whole, unliterary scholastic philosophers arrived—even as our time is the period of unliterary science; and although classical scholars may now know more than their predecessors of the eighteenth century, nevertheless interest in classical literature is on the wane, and the classics are less generally read and have less effect upon educated men than heretofore.

But Petrarch, in contrast with Hildebert of Lavardin and John of Salisbury, lived at the opening of an epoch which was to be intellectually characterized by a renewed, an enthusiastic, a fashionable, modish, almost universal, interest in the classics as veritable fonts of humanity. He and his labors and his fame were borne onwards upon the increasing currents of the coming time. Fate made him a precious pioneer. By reason of his happy timeliness, the fame of him and the effect of him and the inspiration of his example were not lost.

Thus in his Latin studies and Latin writings, Petrarch was a spokesman of the coming time. But beyond his classical virtuosity, through his sonnets and *Canzoni* in Italian, he devised modes of sentiment and the forms of their expression destined to royal fortunes. It was he more than any other who set the sonnet fashion for the following centuries, and within the sonnet form gave expression to those exquisite or precieuse sentiments which became conventions with the writers of love poetry of many nations. He was the main source and inspiration of an enormous sonnet literature in Italy, next in France, and ultimately in England. As the creator of these forms of expression one can find no definite limit to his influence.

II

Boccaccio was a slightly younger contemporary, a devoted friend, and an humble but gifted admirer of Petrarch. While his genius was drenched with his immediate mediaeval antecedents, he went beyond or behind them to grasp the fuller riches of the antique. Still more vitally he turned to the instincts and capacities of his own nature, and absorbed the living currents of his time. His personality and life and labors brilliantly represent his time and place, and with this advantage over Petrarch, that Boccaccio was less self-conscious and quite free from pose. He presents himself in his symbolical and mediaeval elements, in his enthusiastic study of the classics, and in the turning of his genius to life and to the expression of it in the vernacular.

The mediaeval centuries contained many kinds of men,

though we justifiably choose to see mainly the more striking types. We are interested, for instance, in the type which created chivalry and the Arthurian romances, or again in those lines of spiritual energy which blended in the personalities of a St. Bernard, an Aquinas or a Dante. Yet one remembers that if the first part of the *Roman de la Rose* was written by the exquisite De Lorris, the clever and somewhat encyclopaedic second part had for its author that De Meung who has been likened to Voltaire, and may with equal justice be compared with Boccaccio. Both De Meung and Boccaccio employed the mediaeval machinery of presentation, the dream, the vision, the allegory, while both also saw human nature along the level of its actuality. Neither of them dwelt in the *machina,*—the vision or the allegory—which they conventionally used.

That the intellectual conventions and primary mental attitudes of this Florentine were those of the fourteenth century, and the centuries immediately behind it, is evident from his earlier works, which are mediaeval in substance and in the conventions of their construction. One notices the mediaevalism of that *Vita di Dante* in which Boccaccio expressed his admiration for the figure then dominating literary Italy. As Boccaccio was not mystically winged, but well equipped with human hands and feet and eyes, he does not cleave the empyrean with his poet, but makes him walk the earthly levels of the mediaeval meadows, and credits him with motives, romantic, pretty, by no means sublime. Boccaccio's own vocabulary was then full of the words and phrases of the *Commedia*.[21] And at the close of life, when his last labor was to deliver his lectures or *Commento* on it, he adopts scholastically what probably was Dante's own explanation of his purpose, when considering a commentary upon his own poem. The causes, says Boccaccio, of the *Commedia,* are the material, the formal, the efficient and the final. The first of these, which is to say the *subject* of

---

[21] E.g. the "infiniti guai," at the opening of the *Fiammetta,* and shortly after in the lover's words: "O donna, tu sola se' la beatudine nostra."

the poem, is twofold, literal and allegorical. It is, "according to the literal sense, the state of souls after the body's death, taken simply . . . while, according to the allegorical sense, it is how man, mounting or falling through his free will, is bound to the justice which rewards and punishes." So he proceeds with the rest, saying at last that "the final cause is to help those who are living in the present life, to pass from a state of misery to one of felicity."[22] One may add, that this ardent admirer transferred to Dante himself the Dantesque and mediaeval appellative of Aristotle, calling him in the *Amorosa Visione,* "il signor d'ogni savere."

That Boccaccio's way of handling the classics, and presenting their extracted substance in exhaustive compilations, was still mediaeval, may be seen in his *De Casibus Virorum Illustrium,* which shows the fatal turns of fortune through a line of ancient worthies, beginning with Adam; likewise in his *De claris Mulieribus,* a companion treatise; and finally in his vast *Genealogiae deorum gentilium,* in which he endeavors to satisfy his insatiate interest in mythology. No work of Petrarch shows such exhaustive learning. Yet it is clear that Petrarch appreciated the classics more intelligently than this younger man who equalled him in diligence of study and in zeal to extend the knowledge of them. There was no more eager searcher after manuscripts than Boccaccio.

Theoretically, Boccaccio joined with his friend in placing the writing of Latin above Italian composition. But, in fact, more genially and truly than Petrarch he recognized the value and dignity of the *volgare,* and accepted it as a worthy vehicle of narrative and thought, as Dante fortunately had done. Here lay the true progress of Boccaccio, wherein a realization that the classics also drew from life may have helped him on. Looking to life, drawing from life, Boccaccio knew that the *volgare* alone had the living power to depict it. In this he was not "mediae-

22 *Commento,* Cap. I in Moutier's Ed. I, pp. 3-4.

val"; no man is when he goes straight to the life about him.

This great advance did not come suddenly, or in Boccaccio's early years, when he wrote his first poems in the *volgare*. They and their author were still entangled in the acceptance and conventional treatment of conventional subjects. It was not so much that the subjects were timeworn, as that his treatment of them still subscribed to the old notions; for there was life and beauty in the old story of Flore and Blanchfleur, of Troilus and Cressid, or of Palamon and Arcite. The poems made by Boccaccio from these tales, the *Filocolo, Filostrato,* and *Teseide,* have still too much rhetoric and convention, with too little of life's closer observation. Imitation and the old ideas enveloped him most appallingly in his *Amorosa Visione.* In form it copied, parodied rather, the *Divina Commedia,* and in contents was an encyclopaedic "Hall of Fame," in which the author beheld every imaginable person belonging to classical and biblical antiquity, or to the mediaeval time, and also the whole company of allegorical personifications. The enumerating habit followed him. Even in his prose *Fiammetta,* which so aptly delineated passion, he could not help letting Venus set before his heroine the tale of all the gods and demigods and heroes who had been overcome by love, as an argument why she should not resist it. Nor does she.

That Boccaccio at last should have emerged from these entanglements to write the *Decameron!* Its opening stories still carry conventional moralizings. But as the tales proceed, the author reaches an artistic freedom of his own, and, drawing upon universal life, gives pictures of manifold humanity. His cheerful and facile and abundantly carnal nature did not rise to those spiritual heights which may be just as veritable as the streets and gutters of human life. But, with this qualification, the wide actual world throngs through these tales, the world of men and women, resourceful lovers, clever rogues, shameless villains, caught hot in their doings. Many pretty stories, and stories unabashed, with author and audience ready to laugh at folly and applaud the successful ruse. Throughout, cleverness, quick faculty, *virtus* and *prudentia*, ἀρετή and πινυτή, to go back through Rome even to Homer, win life's prizes and applause. High principle, self-sacrifice, humility, gain scant attention, when not laughed out of court. Boccaccio's world has passion and desire, but not much heart or benevolence. It is not malevolent; but as the author does not let the wish to instruct or benefit deflect his story, or spoil his art, so no one in the tale is stayed from his desire by moral nicety.

Boccaccio did not invent many of the tales; he drew from books and on the cloud of homeless stories floating through the world. But his observation and his art made these stories the amusing things they have proved themselves to be for half a thousand years. The life about him and his quick selecting eye gave matter and form. And then his art,—that was a faculty which sprang from the whole Boccaccio and his entire training. Was he not courtier, man of the world, and lady's man and frequent lover? And was he not as well a careful writer, and a deep student of the Latin classics? If he felt that the *volgare* was the tool of life, did he not utterly admire Latin, and deem it better in itself? Could he not use the life which pulsed in the *volgare,* and yet mould that energy to seemliness, perhaps to the seemliness of the Latin period? This was what he did; nor did he fail to inject in it his own apt sense of fitness. So he built his style. And in that style, so apt if still rotund, and, in Boccaccio's faculty of composition, so disciplined, so slowly won, lay the best humanistic progress, the best which that time or any century after it could gain from the study of the classics: to wit, discipline, sense of form, knowledge of literary effectiveness, even a more excellently trained humanity directed toward self-expression.

Such were to be the results of a broader and more instructed study of the classics. Yet the Italians seem hampered by the constraint of the antique in their own natures, and by its survival in their customs and their environment. It was not the revival of classical studies that checked the Italian literary creativeness. Rather, the strength of the antique survival in the Italian nature through every mediaeval century, had checked creativeness. The revival of classical studies gave academic purpose to this hampering survival. Italian scholars, rather more than those of other lands, were touched with the ambition to write classic Latin. This absorbing purpose impeded the creative imagination. With such a darling of delight as Ariosto the fling of fancy would have its play; but many are the names of those Italian humanists, to whose zeal for the resurrection of the Greek as well as Latin classics we remain indebted, yet in whose own Latin compositions self-conscious purpose ill supplies the place of life. A mediaeval Latin writing might be more alive just because the author used Latin as of course, with little stylistic consciousness.

Through the thirteenth and fourteenth centuries, the Italian cities had advanced in wealth, and in human experience and capacity. Elsewhere, in England for example, such development of human faculty might take the form of sharpened political and theological insight, and address itself to religious reform. But, in Italy, it naturally directed itself to studies relating to the Roman past, which still was in the blood. As the prime Italian intellectual achievement of the twelfth and thirteenth centuries had been the revival of the Roman Law, so now in the fourteenth and fifteenth centuries the finer intellectual energies of the land wound themselves about the classics. If Petrarch was the hierarch of these studies, they were pursued by many other men, in cities less rude, more generally cultured, civilized, *urban,* than the towns across the Alps. Not without reason Petrarch contrasts his Italy with the Scythian barbarism of the north, of devastated France for instance, where nevertheless he found upon his journey groups of Latin scholars.

So, as of course, the great revival, the new florescence of classical studies began in Italy. There it presents itself as an original or indigenous movement, which had not come over the borders from another country; there, also, it was a direct study of the Latin and gradually the Greek authors, an acceptance of their influence unmixed with intrusions from neighboring contemporary peoples. This Italian humanism had thus the purity and originality belonging to priority. But in France, England, Germany, so many suggestions came from Italy that there was always a foreign contemporary flavor or suggestion mingling with the study of the classic writings. Whatever came from Italy, in the fourteenth and fifteenth centuries, was almost as that which was taken from the classic literature of Rome.

Chapter 2

Italian Humanists of the Early Fifteenth Century

UNDOUBTEDLY THE GENERAL CULTURE of the Middle Ages rested upon material conditions. The life of court and camp and town and castle, with the delectable productions of poets, church-builders, sculptors, artists in glass, was supported by the economic situation, if not part of it. Monks in monasteries and the student hordes thronging the universities were fed and clothed, and many of their intellectual needs ministered to, through the same supporting wealth. Nevertheless, the finest flowering of the mediaeval spirit ignored bodily well-being, even ascetically deprecated it. But in the coming time, the forms of intellectual achievement and the Protestant religious movement frankly made much of bodily well-being, and hung upon the increase of wealth and material civilization.

Starting with any mediaeval century, the twelfth for instance, one may observe how the factors in the increase of wealth were identical with the means or conditions of expansion of the human mind. Mental and material elements acted upon each other reciprocally, now appearing as result and again as cause. Intellectual development produced discoveries and alternately sprang from them: dicoveries in knowledge, discoveries of mechanical contrivances like the compass; discoveries regarding building, sculpture, painting, the weaving of textile fabrics; relating to commerce and the routes of commerce, to the extension of the knowledge of the earth's surface through exploration of hitherto unknown lands and seas. All this had as much to do with the improvement of man's physical well-being as with the enlargement of his mind. The maritime discoveries afford the most picturesque illustration. From the time of the Scandinavian and Norman voyages, from the time of the Crusades, from the time of the Genoese and Portuguese explorations of the west coast of Africa, to that of the gradually led up to and grandly accomplished voyages of Columbus and Vasco da Gama, the course of maritime exploration is connected with the intellectual development of Europe, and on the other hand becomes the mightiest of factors in that increase in wealth which amounted to an economic revolution. During the sixteenth century, the money supply in Europe would seem to have been quadrupled; and the increase of gold and silver was matched by the expansion of the mental horizon.

A realization of the growth of wealth and luxury in Italy and Spain and France, not to mention England and Germany, is needed for any proper view of the intellectual progress of the fifteenth and sixteenth centuries. Humanism, the study of the classics, while not necessarily a thing of luxury and ease, will be seen to have advanced with the luxurious adornment of life, made possible through wealth. The prosperity of the Italian cities in the thirteenth and fourteenth centuries was the foundation of the brilliant life and culture of the fifteenth, and the necessary basis for the subsequent progress of humanism, science, and philosophy. Support from wealthy patrons, dynasts, tyrants, successful condittieri, enabled the humanists to prosecute their studies, or gave Leonardo da Vinci opportunity for observation and experiment. The famous arsenal at Venice, with its store of costly machines, proved full of teaching for him, as it did for Galileo.

One recalls the industrial growth of Florence. Her wars and treaties had been inspired by her industrial and commercial needs, the need, for instance, of a sea-port, which was not satisfied till Pisa was captured in 1406. A quick commercial expansion resulted. Before then, however, industrious and intriguing Florence traded vigorously with Bruges and the west of Europe, as well as with the near and further Orient. She had given attention to navigation, and to astronomy and other sciences useful in commerce and manufacture. The woolen industry was well developed. Two of her *Arti maggiori,* (the greater Guilds) were engaged in the finishing of foreign woolens and the making of the cloth itself. When English and Flemish competition impaired this lucrative business, the manufacture of silk was profitably taken up. Lawyers too, and money-changers who became great bankers, assisted in the ordering and extension of her industry and commerce. The city continued dominantly Guelf, and with reason, since great gain and the control of Italian finance came to the Florentines as Bankers to the Holy See.[1]

So, for the fifteenth and sixteenth centuries in western Europe, one sees how closely allied were the expansion of the mental vision and the increase of wealth and material civilization. But regarding this expansion of the mind and the varied advance of thought and knowledge, we meet again the question of the causal antecedence of one phase of intellectual progress, with respect to other phases possibly to be regarded as effects. The apparent stimulus came from the antique letters, including antique philosophy and political enlightenment. Yet in a way, these had been there always, and the palm of precedence might just as well be awarded to the advancing humanity which, with increasing intellectual capacity, turned to them for illumination.

Thus a questionable priority resolves itself into a more likely coöperation. Nevertheless, the intellectual progress of these centuries seems to begin with a renewed study of the classic literature. This led to a more varied philosophy, and even facilitated the advance of science. Hence a survey of the period's intellectual accomplishment prop-

[1] Cf. P. Villari, *I primi due secoli della storia di Firenze,* chap. VI, (Revised Ed. Florence 1905).

erly begins with that revival of classic studies which has come to us as inaugurated by Petrarch and Boccaccio.

One need not retell the story of this revival of antique letters, which has been told so often, and with such charm and pleasurable excitement. Yet some of its more illustrative and personal incidents or phases may be given, and not too briefly, for the subject is beguiling. One passes quite naturally from Petrarch to the younger generation of his followers and admirers. These, with their pupils, included the majority of noted humanists flourishing in the first half of the fifteenth century. Petrarch had never made his home in Florence; but most of Boccaccio's life was passed either there or in the neighboring village of Certaldo. And, before long, Florence, chiefly through the energies and tastes of its citizens, became the centre of the classical revival, and one may say, of the new intellectual eagerness inspiring or accompanying it. The city's prosperity under the rule of an aristocracy of wealth, during the half century or more following Boccaccio's death, led to the same end. That the rich Florentines were keenly interested in the Latin classics, as well as in Christian scholarship and Italian literature, appears from an account, true enough if actually fictitious, of the conversation of a distinguished company assembled at the villa of the merchant prince, Antonio degli Alberti.[2] There is costly food and wine, there is music; stories are told, frequently ending in pleasant riddles; philosophy is discussed and Augustine; Ovid and Livy, and the origins of Florence and Prato; also Dante and Petrarch and Boccaccio; the greatness of these men and the richness and worth of the *volgare* find staunch supporters.

The finer Florentine spirits were constantly meeting for the serious pleasures of study and discussion before the fourteenth century had closed. Among them the name of Luigi de Marsigli should not be forgotten, nor will that of Coluccio Salutato. Both of them had "assisted" at the

2 *Il Paradiso degli Alberti,* ed. A. Wesselofsky, 3 vols. (Bologna, 1867).

storied *conversazione.* The voluminous correspondence of
the latter [3] brings the man and his thoughts before us,
and affords an enlightening picture of a deeply respected
Florentine official and meritorious humanist of the generation immediately following Petrarch.

Born in 1330, Salutato was some twenty-five years
younger than his pole-star of a poet. Educated principally
at Bologna, he fitted himself there for the business of a
notary. He had even then heard of Petrarch, had sent
him verses, and had received a little golden letter in return. Afterwards he moved about through various cities,
and gained experience as a scribe in the papal Curia. He
was forty years old when he came to Florence. For a
while he acted as secretary to the Priori, and in 1375
was made Cancellarius, or, as one might say, Secretary
of the Republic. Until his death thirty years later, he
filled this office, enhancing both its dignity and his own
repute through his abilities and uprightness. He was a
man of presence, somewhat austere in manner, but of
deep, controlled affections. All Italy regarded him highly;
and his official papers, which everywhere were preserved
as models, efficiently upheld the Republic's policy and fortunes in times of stress and conflict with the papacy. His
honor never was impeached, and having trained a family
of noble sons, he left them no ill gotten gains. He was
given a public funeral, and crowned with laurel in his
coffin as a poet. He had composed poems enough; yet
their merits scarcely won for him this crown, but rather
his public services and his reputation as a humanist.

One marks his boundless admiration for Petrarch, his
pietas toward him. The poet was dead; the world of scholarly taste was agog to know about his *Africa*—had he de-
stroyed it, as he had threatened, or had he left directions
for its destruction, as Virgil had ordered the destruction
of the *Aeneid?* No! the "divine *Africa*" still existed, for
the joy and solace of mankind. After urgent efforts, it

[3] *Epistolario di Coluccio Salutati,* Ed. Fr. Novati (4 vols., 1891
sqq.).

was copied and brought to Florence, where the new-made humanistic Cancellarius set himself reverently to expunge such harsh expressions as the poet himself would have remedied, had he lived to perfect his work.

At the news of Petrarch's death, Salutato had added a postscript to a letter he was writing: "I have heard, woe is me! that our Petrarch has migrated to his stars." He soon begins to write more at length about him; for instance, to the Count of Battifolle, somewhat as follows: Since Petrarch lived enough for nature and glory, there was nothing more for him to enjoy among mortals, but only to say with the Doctor to the Gentiles, "I desire to be dissolved and be with Christ." He excelled all in wisdom and learning, and in his matchless *eloquentia,* the *eloquendi facultas,* "from which either prose melody (pro-saica melodia) pours forth with loosened reins, or is constrained by the continuous straits of metres." Divid-ing prose into that which serves debate and that which serves instruction (*contentio* and *sermocinatio,* a division in mediaeval use), the letter maintains that Petrarch in his "Invective against a physician," surpassed the Philip-pics and Catiline orations of Cicero. "Believe me, though someone should contend that Cicero was his equal in oratorical power, yet in the adornment of speech and weight of meaning . . . without any doubt it would be admitted that the parent of Roman eloquence was con-quered by this one of ours." Cicero excelled only in the one form of *eloquentia,* and Virgil in the other: Petrarch, who achieved so gloriously in both, is to be set before either of them. And if Greece should insolently compare herself with Latium, we still have Petrarch to set above them. Besides there are his poems in the *volgare,* in which it is acknowledged that he excelled Dante.[4] All hail! con-summate man—summe vir, cui etiam se tota equare non potest antiquitas!" [5]

4 Probably this was not Salutato's more considered opinion. In Lib. XI, 10, he says at great length that there is nothing greater than the *Commedia.*

5 "—most excellent man, unequalled by all the ancient world." *Epistolario,* Lib. III, Ep. 13 and 15.

Such epistolary rhetoric reveals the writer's mentality. Salutato could worship many gods, though for the time one of them should fill his vision. Later he writes in praise of Virgil, saying: "Placet mihi stilus, quem hactenus nemo versibus adequavit, nec putem posse ad eius altitudinem atque dulcedinem humanis viribus pervenire." [6] Yet still later, in 1379, when Petrarch had been dead for five years, he argues, lengthily as was his wont, that Petrarch is superior to Virgil, and in prose the equal of Cicero. [7]

If Salutato appears stupid, Bruni and Poggio were among his protégés. The latter could not endure that his venerable friend and benefactor should put Petrarch above Cicero and Virgil; and the aged Salutato writes to defend his views. You seem to hold, says he, that no modern can be compared with the ancients. That is easy to answer. But first one should consider the Christians, Origen, Chrysostom, Jerome, and Augustine, the best of all. Would you set Plato or Aristotle or Cicero or Virgil above Augustine? And surely, the Latins were superior to the Greeks. [8]

Such crude comparisons, and the conviction of the superiority of Latin over Greek, of which Salutato knew next to nothing, were not common in the next generation. The letter last referred to is so long and tedious that one loses any likely thread of argument. In it Salutato distinguishes between *sapientia* and *eloquentia,* and argues that Aristotle, Plato, and all the Gentiles were necessarily inferior in *sapientia* to the Christians, and therefore inferior to Petrarch. And if they failed in *sapientia,* their *eloquentia* was vain. He expresses his agreement with Cicero that writing should progress from age to age, and correspond with speech and customs. And, returning to his comparisons, he intimates that in putting Petrarch be-

[6] "I am delighted with his style, which no one has yet been able to attain in verse; nor do I think that human powers alone can reach such heights and such grace."

[7] Ep. Lib. IV, 15 and 20.

[8] Ep. Lib. XIV, 18. Dec. 1405.

fore Cicero and Virgil, he really meant that Petrarch excelled Cicero in verse and Virgil in prose!

Through a small hole, the old man emerges to this
ridiculous conclusion. Was he failing mentally, or just
involved in stupid mental habits? He does not seem foolish when, in a still later letter, he says that we should
not slavishly imitate the ancients. But his head is full of
them; sometimes they mould his own mood or seemingly
living thoughts, or again they are as names which he keeps
waving in his letters. He can argue as to the authorship of
the tragedies ascribed to Seneca, with better knowledge
and acumen than could have been found, say, before Petrarch, and can show a real appreciation of Cicero's
character drawn from his letters; and he wrote frequently
upon questions of textual interpretation. But his critical
knowledge was so incomplete that apparently he took no
exception to the statements of "Dares" and "Dyctys," in
their wretched Trojan forgeries, which the Middle Ages
also had followed. Nor does he feel the absurdity of his
long epistle combatting the charge that Aeneas was not
the *legitimate* son of Venus.[9] He is ready with a string
of names that so long had served as band-horses. He con-
soles a young Count for the death of a father whose writing and speech *redolebat* of the streams of Cicero, the
pointedness of Quintilian, the vehemence of Demosthenes.
He would have the young man lift up his heart;—how
are our minds inflamed for virtue in thinking on the
"Claudios, Fabricios, Curios, Catones, Fabios, Metellos,
Scipiones, Decios, Lucullos et ceteros." And writing to
a prominent citizen of Lucca, he finds him not inferior
to Brutus in one respect, nor to Manlius in another, nor
to Camillus in a third. Coluccio knew himself and the
compass of his mind, when he wrote to Cardinal Orsini,
urging the reading of the good old ancients; for we invent
nothing new, and are but patchers of antique apparel.[10]

9 Ib. V, 18; VIII, 7; X, 9 and 12; XII, 21.
10 Ib. II, 18; III, 17; VI, 4.

Though naturally maintaining that zeal for sacred studies did not call for the banishment of the pagan poets, Salutato was not a pagan, but a serious person, who liked to discuss free will and predestination. He was a man of piety, distinctly recognizing how fraught with dangers were the praise and glory of this world. It was natural that Greeks and Romans should have delighted "ardently in the extinguishable light of glory, and have found it dulcissimum pro gloria mori. But be it far from me, a Christian man, to glory in knowledge which puffeth up, or in anything save the Mediator of God and men." And in the following letter which is an argument for the use of *tu* instead of *vos* when addressing a single person, he says "we are born for glory, eternal glory, not the fragile and fleeting glory of the world." [11]

In sundry letters, written to console Andrea de Volterra for the death of his sons, the antique temper supports Christian sentiments and convictions. These letters were less completely pagan than one written in the early twelfth century by Bishop Hildebert to Henry I of England on the drowning of his son.[12] Salutato borrows thoughts which Scipio and Laelius might express concerning friendship, and blows them up to a thin flame. Yet, beneath these quasi-affectations, classic sentiment had entered and disciplined his nature.

Although this worthy man affected to set Latin above Greek, no one did more to bring to Florence the Greek language and literature, in the person of the excellent Chrysoloras,[13] a Byzantine of quite another class from the charlatans who had imposed on Boccaccio. He was ever quick and generous in aiding the cause of letters; and, in his old age, was like a father to Bruni and Poggio,

11 Ib. IV, 18; VII, 17; VIII, 10 and 11.

12 VIII, 17, 18, 19, cf. XI, 8. See *The Mediaeval Mind*, II, p. 173. In Lib. IX, 9, Salutato mentions Hildebert, Abelard, St. Bernard and other mediaeval worthies, as good letter writers.

13 Lib. IX, 14 (1406) formally invites him to Florence at a salary.

who then enter his life and correspondence. The fifteenth epistle of Liber XIV (Aug. 1405) to Pope Innocent VII, is a hearty and ornate recommendation of Bruni for the post of Apostolic secretary; and the same Liber contains many letters to the young Poggio, affectionate and filled with good advice. Poggio as well as Bruni called him "father and teacher"; and a picture of the old man is given in Bruni's *"Libellus de Disputationum etc. usu,"*[14] written in 1401, when the author was about thirty.

This little book enlightens us as to the change which had come over the younger generation of scholars. It opens with the friends, Bruni, Niccolo and de Rossi, going to see the venerable man, just as Scipio and Laelius go to see the aged Cato in Cicero's *de Senectute*. The nominal subject of their talk is the value of discussion of literary themes. Niccolo opens with a harsh note: "I fail to see, Coluccio, how in these dregs of time (in hac faece temporum, a common humanistic phrase) and in this great dearth of books, anyone can acquire the faculty of discussing." Our ancestors, he continued, preserved Cassiodorus, and suffered Cicero to perish. Then, assailing the ignorant present-day followers of Aristotle, he deplores the condition of philosophy, dialectic, grammar, and rhetoric.

Salutato is less pessimistic: if we have lost much, much is left; and consider the pre-excellence of Dante, Petrarch, and Boccaccio. Niccolo will not hear of praising them, whom the crowd praises. Dante showed his ignorance in giving a white beard to Cato, who died at the age of forty-eight; and his treatment of Brutus was very bad. He should be left out of any "concilium litteratorum." As for Petrarch, his long looked for *Africa* was born a "ridiculus mus"; his friends were sick of it; it was a poor performance. Enough could be said against Boccaccio too.

Smiling as was his wont, Salutato postpones the defense

14 Printed in T. Klette, *Beiträge zur Ges. und Lit. der Italienischen Gelehrtenrenaissance*, (Greifswald 1888).

of these men to the next day, when the friends meet again at his house. The task of defense is laid on Bruni; but Niccolo says that he had spoken as he had only to hear what Salutato would say; in fact he admires them all, and he proceeds to praise each in turn, but stands to it that he does not care for the *Africa* or Petrarch's *Bucolics*.

These younger men had thrown off the Petrarch spell,[15] and had discarded certain of Salutato's stupid notions. They knew more; some of them knew Greek, and had read Greek authors. They had thus gained a better perspective. They wrote easier Latin than Salutato or Boccaccio or Petrarch. They and their generation were eagerly engaged in the search for manuscripts, and their efforts were rewarded.[16]

Florence was still the hearth and home of humanists; and it was of lasting import for the cause of learning that Chrysoloras came there to lecture. We turn to Bruni's story of the call he felt to study Greek, told in his *History of his own times in Italy*.[17] The closing years of the fourteenth century are referred to:

"Then first came a knowledge of Greek, which had not been in use among us for seven hundred years. Chrysoloras the Byzantine, a man of noble birth and well versed in Greek letters, brought Greek learning to us. When his country was invaded by the Turks, he came

[15] After writing the lives of Dante and Petrarch, Bruni compares the two. He speaks of Petrarch's greater faculty of keeping the friendship of princes, and comments thus: "E certo il vivere in reputazione ed in vita onorato da tutti i Signori e Popoli, non fu senza gradissima virtù, e sapienza e costanza." This was written about 1436.

[16] The exciting story of the search and rescue of manuscripts of the classics is told by J. A. Symonds in his "Revival of Learning," and more circumstantially in G. Voigt's *Wiederbelebung des Klassischen Alterthum's*.

[17] *Commentarius rerum suo tempore in Italia gestarum*, by Leonardus Aretinus (of Arezzo) called Bruni; Muratori, *Script*. T. 19, pp. 914 sqq. Bruni was born about 1370 and died in 1444. The passage quoted begins on page 920 of Muratori.

by sea, first to Venice. The report of him soon spread, and he was cordially invited and besought and promised a public stipend, to come to Florence and open his store of riches to the youth. I was then studying Civil Law, but . . . I burned with love of academic studies, and had spent no little pains on dialectic and rhetoric. At the coming of Chrysoloras I was torn in mind, deeming it shameful to desert the law, and yet a crime to lose such a chance of studying Greek literature; and often with youthful impulse I would say to myself: 'Thou, when it is permitted thee to gaze on Homer, Plato and Demosthenes, and the other poets, philosophers, orators, of whom such glorious things are spread abroad, and speak with them and be instructed in their admirable teaching, wilt thou desert and rob thyself? Wilt thou neglect this opportunity so divinely offered? For seven hundred years, no one in Italy has possessed Greek letters; and yet we confess that all knowledge is derived from them. How great advantage to your knowledge, enhancement of your fame, increase of your pleasure, will come from an understanding of this tongue? There are doctors of civil law everywhere; and the chance of learning will not fail thee. But if this one and only doctor of Greek letters disappears, no one can be found to teach thee.' Overcome at length by these reasons, I gave myself to Chrysoloras, with such zeal to learn, that what through the wakeful day I gathered, I followed after in the night, even when asleep."

Bruni gives the names of fellow students, who studied Greek with more or less pertinacity and success. Some of them were to be noted humanists; but none of them was as good a Greek scholar, or did as much with his knowledge of Greek, as Bruni himself. The fame of Greek, even the enthusiasm for it, was spreading among Italian students of the humanities; but its study presented more difficulties than opportunities; and through the first half of the fifteenth century, more humanists talked about

Greek than seriously attempted to acquire it. Of those
who did, not a few were discouraged by the difficulties
of the script and language, and the lack of competent
teachers and manuscripts. Bruni himself collected Greek
manuscripts, as he had to in order to pursue his studies;
but he never carried his search into the East. It was
Giovanni Aurispa who returned from Constantinople to
Venice in 1423, with a grand load of manuscripts; and
a few years after him, Filelfo, of many-sided repute,
brought not a few, and did much to advance the study
of Greek literature in Italy. If the renewed study of the
Latin Classics, with the unearthing of new manuscripts,
proceeded with zeal and pleasurable excitement, and became the darling pursuit of many a man of wealth, one
may imagine the expectation aroused at the prospect of
a new and greater world of Greek literature; an expectation which was not to be disappointed.

So, in Bruni's time, an acquaintance with Greek was
hardly more common in Italy than a knowledge of San-
scrit is at present in America. The difference was in the
hope of enlightenment, which no one expects from San-
scrit, but which those men of the fifteenth century fer-
vently looked for from the Greek gospel of knowledge.
Of course, all knowledge of the language, even that possessed by the very facile Bruni, was imperfect, and his
translations faulty. But his accomplishment was extraordinary, and the spirit of his labors admirable. He translated many of Plutarch's Lives, Plato's *Phaedo, Gorgias,
Phaedrus, Crito,* and *Apologia;* ten books of Aristotle's
Ethics, eight books of his *Politics,* two books of his *Eco-
nomics;* then Aeschines against Ctesiphon and Demosthenes' *de Corona,* and something more from Demosthenes with bits from Aristophanes, and extracts from
Xenophon. In a letter to his occasionally rasping friend,
Niccolo Niccoli,[18] Bruni writes that his love for Plato

18 Lib. I, ep. 8, in L. Mehus's edition of Bruni's letters—*Leon-
ardi Bruni Aretini Epistolarum Libri VIII,* Florence 1741, 2 vols.
(There are in fact ten *libri* in this edition.)

grows as he advances with his translations; and he is grateful to "Coluccio patri ac praeceptori meo" for urging the work upon him.

"There is in Plato the utmost urbanity, the finest method of reasoning, and subtlety; while the abundant and divine opinions of the disputants are given with marvellous pleasantness and an incredible fluency of phrase. His is the utmost facility of speech, with an abundance of that admirable χάρις, as the Greeks call it. There is neither sweating nor violence; everything is said as by a man who holds words and their laws in his power. . . . Such a one indeed is Plato among the Greeks, and unless I show him such to the Latins, let them be sure that he is made worse through my fault, and not think they are reading Plato, but my ineptitudes. I promise to labor to keep that from happening; I do not promise to succeed, for I would not dare make any such promise. But unless I am mistaken, I will warrant you, that you shall read your Plato without annoyance, and, I will add, with the greatest pleasure; which I think neither Calcidius, nor the other [translator] who has carefully withheld his name, has enabled you to do. They perhaps set about it in one way, and I in another. For they, departing from Plato, have followed syllables and figures of speech; but I adhere to Plato, whom I imagine to myself as knowing Latin, so that he can judge, and be a witness to his translation; and I translate in such wise as I know will please him best. In the first place, I preserve all his ideas, so as not to depart from them in the least. Then if I can render him word for word, without impropriety or absurdity, I choose that way. But if that is impossible, I am not afraid of falling into the crime of lèse majesté, if, when I have kept the idea, I depart ever so little from the words, so as to avoid absurdity. For Plato himself presently orders me to do this, since he, who is most elegant of speech among the Greeks, does not wish, among the Latins, to appear absurd. Following these principles, unless I do as I promise, I do not object to being thrown into the oven."

In the next generation, Bruni's translations of Plato were to be superseded by Ficino's; and in his lifetime, he had many a battle to fight over his renderings of Aristotle. He vows that he never added one jot or tittle to Aristotle's meaning, and had differed from former translators only after deep consideration. Let his critics first understand Greek and know the force of its words, upon which he has spent more than eighteen years of study, and has overlooked no point of brilliancy in the Greek tongue. "Besides Aristotle, so much from Plato, Demosthenes, Plutarch, Xenophon, have we translated, that we have become veterans in that art, not tyros!" Bruni admired Aristotle even as a writer: "I do not see how anyone could write more suitably or pleasantly or fluently upon those matters which Aristotle treated. . . . Surely, if anyone should throw dirt on one of Giotto's pictures, I could not stand it. How then do you think it is with me, when I see Aristotle's works, more precious than any picture, defiled with such dirt of a translation!" [19]

Bruni's letters, though less brilliant than Poggio's, are pleasant reading. He wrote many books, among which he may have attached most value to his *History of Florence*. Innocent VII called him, while still little more than a protégé of Salutato's, to the post of papal secretary. The pope was taken aback at his youthful appearance, but was amply reassured by the first letters which he composed, as Bruni recounts to his old friend and master.[20] His clear and sprightly epistolary style attracts one now; the writer was very much awake. Passing over the Eastern Alps from Trent to the Council of Constance, this papal secretary was impressed with the asperities of the way: "Mountains so great and cliffs so high, such

19 Lib. X, Ep. 26; IV, Ep. 22. cf. VII, 4 and 7.
20 Lib. I, Ep. 1 and 2.

ridges, peaks and summits, such giants everywhere rise up, that one marvels exceedingly what that parent and framer of the world, Nature, was after when she made them. Horror, indeed, and awe held me as I gazed on those eternal and everlasting masses, and I cannot recall them now without a shudder."[21] Doubtless Bruni felt this; he is still close to the classic attitude toward mountains, for which the Middle Ages also had no love.

Bruni appreciated the humane influence to be gained from classic studies. "Let your application have a two-fold end," he writes to a youth, "the one the knowledge of letters, the other an understanding of those things which pertain to life and manners, which on that account are called *humanitatis studia,* because they perfect and equip the man." He was finely conscious of the inner significance of language, the meaning to be read between the lines: "Intent is grasped not only from words, which may be feigned, but from the expression in the face and eyes of the speaker. . . . I also seem to notice the same in the letters of a good writer . . . in which, besides words and sound, there is something behind, a tacit indication of the mind, which, as from the movement of a speaker's eyes, you may catch, in a writer, from the very vibration of his discourse." [22]

Bruni held his papal secretaryship under successive popes; but he closed his life as chancellor of Florence, as his master Coluccio before him; and, like Coluccio, as he lay in his coffin, "indutus sericam vestem calore ferru-gineo," he was crowned with laurel by Mannetti, who gave a long oration upon his career and virtues; to which Poggio added a shorter and admirable one.[23]

The cleverest of all these early Latin-writing, Greek-studying scholars was this Poggio Bracciolini.[24] Although

[21] Lib. IV, Ep. 3.
[22] Lib. VI, Ep. 6; VII, Ep. 3.
[23] These orations are printed in Mehus's edition of Bruni's letters, Vol. I, pp. LXXXIX-CXXVI.
[24] There is a good monograph on Poggio, E. Walser, *Poggius Florentinus,* (Berlin 1914), which has been translated into English.

he spent most of his life in the service of the Curia at Rome, he belongs to the Florentine group, through birth in the neighborhood of Florence, through early education, and through life-long association. Born in 1380 of impoverished parents, he came when but a boy to the city, where Salutato became interested in him, and soon treated him as a son. He made friends, above all with that collector of friends as well as books, the excellent Latinist, Niccolo Niccoli, who lent him his countenance and books and money. He heard Chrysoloras lecture; but at that early age had still to devote himself to Latin and to earning a living by copying manuscripts. When twenty-three, he went to Rome to begin a long and wellpaid, though often interrupted, service of the Curia. But his mind clung to Florence, whether his body was at Rome, or in England, or at Constance, Baden or St. Gall. And afterwards in the Florentine *contado,* when he was rich, and the father of two families, he still would build his villa, and fill it with books and broken antique statues, coins and gems and other paraphernalia of a fifteenth century Italian lover of the classics. Florence in her turn honored him; sent him her citizenship when far away in Constance, recognized his quickness to use that pen of his in her defense, and at the end, when he was seventy-three, pressed the office of Chancellor upon him. He died six years after.

In the meanwhile, what a life of student energy had been his! how had he as a hound hunted out manuscripts, freeing them from their dungeons (ergastula) in German cloisters, and restoring more than one classic to actual life. In this hunt he was *facile princeps,* rescuing Quintilian's *Institutes* in St. Gall, and Valerius Flaccus' *Argonautica,* copying them with his own skilled hand. To his credit also should be placed Lucretius, Ammianus Marcellinus, and some of Cicero's orations. He also proved his scholar's intelligence in his ceaseless copying of ancient inscriptions from the monuments, which he recognized as a source of sure contemporary information. And à propos of Poggio, one may remark how naturally classical studies joined with an interest in antiquities of all kinds, with a love for old heads and broken statues, which were also beautiful; and so with the love of visible, sensual beauty, and all things ministering to it. Thus letters were at one with the love of beauty, luxury, and gorgeous living, which one associates with the Italian quattrocento and cinquecento.

Some of Poggio's letters strike us as rhetoric; but often they are delightful, and usually are written in bright, easy Latin, yet with the constant sufficient correctness of a great scholar and litterateur. Well known is his letter telling of the life of Baden, with men and women enjoying themselves socially in the baths. The next epistle is renowned for its narrative of the trial and defense and burning of Jerome of Prague at the Council of Constance, where the martyr heretic dies with the constancy of a Cato, an admirable sight. Again how colloquial Poggio can be—writing to his closest friend: "Quid mihi agendum fuisse existimas, mi Nicole? Constitue te in locum meum:" —put yourself in my place.[25] And what eagerness and impatience fill his page when he scents a new manuscript to be unearthed—in one case the supposed manuscript of Livy; hurry! hurry! pants the letter; get Cosimo to put up the money; get it quick! In this case, he was chasing an *ignis fatuus*. And so he writes and writes, about getting books and books and books, from this and that other German monk or monastery; and he can be sharp enough —why mince words with a friend? as he says to Niccolo: "De libris Germanis nil dicam amplius, nisi me non dormire more tuo, sed vigilare." [26]

Obviously these people, Poggio above all, gave themselves over utterly to collecting books and to classical studies, as men had not done in the Middle Ages. Poggio and Bruni were reputed to be pagans. Italy in their time had no objection to such, hating only heretics. Poggio and

25 This is Ep. I, 11, of Vol. I of Tonelli's edition. The two others precede it.
26 Ep. III, 1.

his friends do not play, as in the Middle Ages, at making all knowledge the handmaid of theology; yet he knows well the phrase, parens et regina scientiarum omnium. Even Poggio has not quite thrown over the Fathers, will at least read them in default of other occupation; in London, for example, whither he had gone, and had been disappointed in his hopes of emolument. There he reads Augustine, and the homilies of Chrysostom in translation. There also he had three months' leisure for Aristotle, turning over his works to see what was in each—reason enough for studying Greek (in which Poggio never was proficient), to know this man in his own tongue, who in another tongue is "elinguis et absurdus." For an expositor, he had Thomas Aquinas, "virum egregium et fecundum." But he returns quickly to Chrysostom and Augustine, wishing to read Augustine on Paul and Matthew: "nam, pace aliorum dixerim, hic vir longe humero supereminet omnes." [27] "Hic vir" is Augustine, and this letter shows how that great Father could hold his own with Poggio, as he had half dominated Petrarch.[28]

Poggio says that the English monasteries had few books to interest him; he saw catalogues containing nothing "dignum studiis humanitatis." Curiously enough, in the same letter he evinces qualms: he cannot adjust his conduct with his principles; even his interests waver. "The sacred books which I have read, and daily read, have cooled my early studium humanitatis, to which, as you know, I have been devoted from boyhood. For the foundations of these studies are vain, partly false;—all vanity! But the foundation of sacred eloquence is truth, which lost, we can hold and do nothing good." He adds, "If you think I have mended my ways, they are worse than ever." But on his fiftieth birthday, he writes to Niccolo that he will seek *gradually* a better sort of life.[29]

---

[27] "For if I may speak with the leave of the others, this man stands head and shoulders above all contenders."

[28] Ep. II, 16; I, 6 & 8.

[29] Ep. I, 13; IV, 5.

One may smile! Poggio's morals were weak enough, though at the age of fifty-five he gave up his mistress, from whom he is said to have had fourteen children, to take a fresh young wife. He was true to his friends, and grateful; but a vile reviler of his enemies, as was the custom of his tribe. Likewise he hunted the emoluments of life and learning; and none equalled him in turning dedications of his writings into money. His *Facetiae* were more often foul than funny. But he was quite of his time, and a fine scholar, to whose zeal for rescuing manuscripts the world owes much.

One cannot speak at length of all the men composing this chief group of early humanists, whose hearth and home was Florence, and whose Maecenas was Cosmo dei Medici. One feels that they were very happy in their enthusiasms. The antique world was a sort of new world for them, newly discovered by them, as it seemed; for they had come to it with such a young new interest; and an interest which in the volume and diffusion and effect of its energy was new in fact. So they felt themselves happily exploring a land unexplored and full of fascinations, full of promise. Their way of life was also new. They did not live in monasteries, nor cluster around Cathedral schools, or hold chairs at universities. They were *literati*, secretaries to cities, to despots, to popes, court scribes, court poets. But among themselves they formed a band, not of brothers, often of hateful foes, but still of men united in their enthusiasms and pursuits. They helped each other enormously. No one of them could have done as much as he did to advance classical scholarship, had not the others aided him; each to each was a tap of information, a lending library, sometimes a source of cash. Those who did not produce much themselves, like Niccolo Niccoli and Ambrosio Traversari, were pivots around whom the others profitably circled. Niccolo Niccoli, a fat little man and autocratic Latinist, is spoken of by Cortesius of the next Florentine generation as one "who gained great glory through cultivating the friendships of the most learned men." He had the best library in

Florence; of its eight hundred volumes, two hundred were in lending in 1437, when he expired devoutly, in the arms of his friend Traversari, the General of the Order of Camalduli. The voluminous collected correspondence of the latter, comprising his own and his friends' letters, serves to bring these men into a group.[30]

As monk and General of his Order, Traversari was a prelate active in ecclesiastical intrigues, and a pillar of conventional piety; but as a man and humanist, he was a vivacious companion, an eager student, and an aid to others. He was worried often by religious compunctions, as in his work at translating the heathen historian of heathen philosophy, Diogenes Laertius. In his own compositions he endeavored to avoid profane citations! He sends to Pope Eugenius IV St. Bernard's *De Consideratione,* as an apt book for a new pope; he is much interested in Greek, and in books, books, books. Also a great reader of the Church Fathers, with a predilection for Lactantius because of his Ciceronian style, and for Athanasius as the rock of orthodoxy. Admiration for that "eximius vir" so holds him, as he says, "ut ab eo divelli non possim." [31] He will devote himself to that "igneo ac coelesti homini," [32] when he can command time. The letters to his close friend Niccolo are generally interesting. A number of them are taken up with his delightful humanistic journey to Rome, and to Venice, Ferrara, Mantua, Ravenna. He stays at the monasteries of his Order and rummages them for manuscripts; he also looks at the antique curiosities of each town: at Ravenna he admires the churches (templa) and many-colored marble columns, and all the mosaics; at Venice, Ciriaco shows him his coins.[33]

The man last named, Ciriaco of Ancona, is known to fame as the tireless, fearless explorer of antique sites, and

---

[30] *Ambrosius Traversarius Camaldunensis,—Epistolae, Vita* &c., ed. by L. Mehus (Florence 1749).

[31] "that I cannot be drawn away from him."

[32] "ardent and heaven-inspired man."

[33] Lib. VIII, ep. 12 and 42-54.

collector of gems and coins, statues and manuscripts, and all sorts of information from places far and difficult.[34] It were a long task to describe his journeys. He was a trader with a passion for exploration, and gained his knowledge and his education as he travelled, even his Latin and Greek. In Rome he visits antique temples, theatres, palaces, baths, triumphal arches, aqueducts as well, and bridges; he makes drawings of columns, and copies inscriptions. He takes ship for Byzantium, and searches for antiquities in Chios, and collects Greek and Latin inscriptions. He visits Rhodes and then Beirut and Damascus, everywhere buying, both as connoisseur and trader, manuscripts and bronzes, coins and gems, any object of antiquarian interest. He visited Adrianople; and afterwards ranged Italy through and through, from Sicily to the northern bounds: he travelled in Dalmatia, Greece, Egypt, visited Crete: it were hard to say where his restless feet did not tread. He appears in humanistic circles, with antiquities to show or sell, and all manner of information (some of it wrong) to impart. His scholarship might be questioned,—that of the self-taught man is likely to be peccable; but he was a well-known and interesting personality. In spite of his faulty knowledge, his collections of inscriptions were of great value.

There was another and more important man, who wandered also, or at least often changed his abode, not from love of exploration, but from restlessness and the difficulties caused by his insolence. This was Filelfo,[35] a man of much learning for his time. He had lived and studied in Constantinople, and had married a Greek wife. In 1427, when not yet thirty years old, he returned from the East,

[34] See G. Voight, *Wiederbelebung* &c., I, p. 269 sqq. (3rd Ed. 1891).

[35] On Filelfo, see Voight, *Wiederbelebung* etc., I, 348 sqq. (3rd Ed.); G. Benadduci, *Prose e poesie volgari di Francesco Filelfo* (Ancona 1901); E. Legrand, *Cent-dix lettres grecques de François Filelfe,* (Paris 1892); T. Klette, *Die griechische Briefe des Franciscus Philelphus,* (Greifswald 1890).

landing at Venice. Well equipped with Greek, he taught there for a while, making a sensation, as he says. About two years afterwards, having tried various ruses to secure a high salary, he came to Florence, at the invitation of Niccolo and Traversari, and under the patronage of Cosimo and other great ones. Besides his Greek accomplishments, he was one of the best of Latin writers in prose and metre. He was to lecture on Livy and Cicero, and Terence, Thucydides, Xenophon and the *Iliad.* His lectures drew great audiences, and he gave hours at home on the humanities, all most successfully. His friendship was sought by the best men. But his head began to strike the clouds a little overmuch; the earth could hardly hold him. He fell out with the temperamental Niccolo—a bad man to fall out with—and sundry others. Cosimo and his brother showed estrangement. In 1433 a revolt of the nobles brought Cosimo to prison. Filelfo spoke out, and urged his death. Cosimo was exiled, but recalled to power within the year, and Filelfo fled advisedly. Some months afterwards a bravo attempted his life in Sienna. The feud was on, the literary feud, with Poggio the chief gladiator on the other side: the weapons ink and filth. Foul as were the mutual accusations, they were not all calumnies. We will not take up this oft-told story. After many decades, when Cosimo had long been dead, Filelfo, reconciled and pardoned by the Medici, returned to Florence a man of eighty-three. It was in the summer; the heat and fatigue of the journey were too much for him. He died as the result. He had done much in Greek as well as Latin prose and verse, and in the *volgare* too.

It is necessary to speak more particularly of Lorentius Valla, unquestionably the hardest thinker and closest scholar that had so far appeared among the Italian humanists. Alfonso of Arragon had made good by force of arms his claim to the Kingdom of Sicily and Naples. He adopted the humanistic fashions of the time in Italy, by showing a constant interest in the classics, having them read to him in translations daily after dinner. He cultivated the society of the learned, and was a patron of those men whose writings should immortalize his deeds and enhance the glory of his reign. Lorentius Valla attached himself to the King in the midst of a campaign. He accompanied him to Naples, and for some years dwelt beneath his aegis, serving him in various literary capacities.

Valla loved to call himself a Roman, although he seems to have been born in Piacenza in 1407. But he passed his youth in Rome, and his early manhood, enjoying there the society and instruction of Bruni, Poggio, and the Greek scholar Aurispa, who had brought his fund of learning and his store of books from Constantinople. Valla was never at his best in Greek, but he possessed a close knowledge of classic Latin, a powerfully reasoning mind, and a temper none too sweetly combative, when he left Rome in 1431. He first taught in Pavia, there attacking both the dialecticians and the jurists. Then he stayed transiently in Milan and Genoa, Ferrara and Mantua, and at last more permanently in Naples, under Alfonso's protection, which he needed.

For Valla did not content himself with piling factitious scorn on rival humanists; he attacked long-held acceptances, and made himself a danger to papal pretensions, if not to Christian morals. With all his devotion to Latin letters, his mind was destructively and constructively critical, and recalcitrant against authority. Curiously enough, in part from an instinct to combat received opinion, Valla maintained the superiority of Quintilian as a rhetorician over Cicero; he later was to assert the superiority of Demosthenes over Cicero as an orator. He stands out among his fellows as an absolute classicist.[36]

The humanist theory, beginning with Petrarch, was to contemn the post-classical and mediaeval changes in Latin, and insist upon conformity to classical models. Yet the practice had been looser, and many current usages were

[36] The works of Valla, except the *Elegantiae*, are difficult to come by. I have gained much from Vahlen's excellent essay on him, in Almanach der Kaiserl. Akad. der Wissenschaften, Vienna, XIV Jahrg. 1864, pp. 183 sqq.

accepted. Valla alone, with strenuous consistency and unique grammatical insight, insisted upon adherence to classical correctness in practice; and proceeded by grammatical analysis to distinguish between classical and all aberrant forms. He set forth these principles with ample illustration in his *Elegantiae* of the Latin tongue, a work occupying him for years, and containing the closest consideration of the meanings and proper use of words. No work of the period evinces such profound reverence for the ancient language of the Romans, *nostrorum majorum,* an ancestorship which Valla held to as a faith. The *Praefatio* proclaims the benign conquest of Europe by the Latin tongue, when arms indeed had failed the Romans: Magnum ergo Latini sermonis sacramentum est:

"Great therefore is the saving power—the sacrament —of the Latin speech, great surely its divinity, which is preserved these many centuries among foreigners, among barbarians, among enemies, scrupulously and religiously, so that we Romans should not grieve, but rejoice, while the whole listening earth should glory. We have lost Rome, we have lost empire, we have lost dominion, not by the fault of us, but of the times; nevertheless, in virtue of this more splendid dominion, we reign until now in a large part of the world."

Rome is indeed captured by the Gauls, he continues, through the horrid decay of Latinity; which this book shall do its share in re-establishing. So far the preface to Book I. The preface to the next book reviles the Latinity of those who came after Donatus, Servius and Priscian—"to whom I ascribe this much, that whoever after them wrote something of Latin (aliquid de Latinitate), would seem to stammer: of those untaught ones, the first and most arrogant is Isidore." The preface to Book III takes a grammarian's view of jurisprudence, agreeing with Quintilian, that "every legal right rests on the interpretation of words, or on the distinction of right and wrong." The preface to the next book turns against those who despise classical learning. Some years later, in 1455, Valla delivered an inaugural *Oratio* in Rome, at the opening of the academic year, taking for his theme the great value of the Latin tongue, which, universally diffused, spreads and preserves knowledge, and enables all men to build together the tower of knowledge understandingly, and not as at Babel.[37]

If Valla's *Elegantiae* laid the foundations of modern classical philology, they also disclosed the quality of their author, his intellectual method, and the sequence of his intellectual activities. He was fundamentally a philologist and grammarian; and it is from the discipline of his analysis of the Latin language that he passes on to criticize the loose or empty thinking obfuscating the minds of contemporaries. In all branches of thought, it is his way to reach greater clarity by analyzing the meanings of words, or again by discovering the impossibilities hinging upon the inconsistencies of statement. So this incisive questing spirit, from the suggestions of a scientific philology, proceeded to attack grammarians, literati, jurists, dialecticians and philosophers, and monks. By sifting the exact from the loose, realities from falsities, he passes to broader criticism, historical or philosophical. Throughout, he shows himself as inconsiderate of other men's opinions as he was considerate of fact.

A true Valla note is struck in a letter touching his old friend Bruni: "I have read through his *Laudation of Florence,*—plenam levitatis et supinitatis. . . . He speaks as if he expected no one to reply to him and much less that anyone should not assent to his absurdities. He would have Florence the heir of the imperium of the Roman people, as if Rome herself were extinct! . . . The style is lax and fluid and enervated, lacking dignity and character, and in many places speaking unlatinly, not to say corruptly." [38]

This hard-headed Valla, so critical of Bruni's patriotic

37 Text published by Vahlen, *L. Vallae tria opuscula,*—Sitz-ber. Phil. Hist. Classe, Vienna Acad. 1869, B'd 62 pp. 93 sqq.

38 To Petrus Candidus (cir. 1435), taken from Barozzi e Sabbadini, *Studi sul Panormita e sul Valla* (Florence 1891).

foolishness, can readily be imagined declaring that Hector and Aeneas, even Rinaldo, were imaginary persons; or we hear him entering upon a critical discussion of the Roman legends, and pointing out inconsistencies in Livy; as in his *Emendationes sex librorum T. Livii de secundo bello punico.* He proceeded more hardily in the interests of Alfonso, as well as truth, to show by lengthy analysis that "Constantine's Donation" was a later forgery. [39] His patron's protection was needed when he was attacked in Naples by the Inquisition, on many grounds, and among others for impugning the accepted view that the Apostles successively enunciated the clauses of the "Apostles' Creed."

There were plenty of other grounds. Valla's quest of truth, and of solid reasons even to support alleged other-worldly thinking, rode rather roughshod over timehonored acceptances as well as interests. The sequence of his writings is not certain. But it was not far from 1447, and when the desire to see Rome again was strong in this Roman fosterling, that he produced his critical *In Novum Testamentum adnotationes,* in which he sought to hark back to the Greek original, and to criticize the Vulgate translation from the invidious vantage ground of a closer philological investigation. He also noted certain inconsistencies among the Gospels.[40]

Only a little less revered than the Vulgate, were the dialectic traditions of the universities; and by attacking these—even the Ten Categories!—Valla made himself obnoxious to the scholastics of his time, whose hate he also drew by the contempt he poured on them, in his book of *Dialecticorum Disputationum.* A veritable pruning of dialectic, *repastinatio* as his sub-title called it, was this writing, which should show how simple an affair was logic

---

[39] *De falso credita et ementita Constantini donatione Declamatio.*

[40] Erasmus was the first really to appreciate and indeed appropriate many of Valla's suggestions. See Vol. II, Chap. 2.

really; much simpler than grammar, if only hair-splitting dialecticians would let it stay so.

But before this book had appeared, indeed before he ever came to Naples, he had made himself suspect to serious people by his famous *De Voluptate,* in which, following Epicurus, he showed that man's highest good lay in a tranquil mind; or, rather, perhaps he did, for he seemed to let Christian teaching triumph in the end. Yet through the work, arguments setting sense-pleasure above all are given with enthusiasm, and may have been intended to prove a valid human truth.[41] At all events, Valla was a hardy reasoner in this book, as well as in his *De libero arbitrio;* and these works seem to have had their effect on the great Leibnitz.

None of these writings stirred such ecclesiastic hate as the dialogue *De Professione Religiosorum,*[42] against the monks. Valla, as one of the speakers, denies them the name of *religiosi,* since they do not make a *religio* but a *secta,* a word corresponding to the Greek αιεσις, and pregnant with the detestable innuendo of this derivation. The *Frater* answers. But the course of the argument invalidates his claims to a superior mode of life; an analysis of his statements shows them to prove nothing. Valla prefers to twist his opponent up in his own misused words, rather than put forward counter allegations. Naturally, the monk's side is feebly stated, and Valla's cleverly. Yet some years later, in an *Apologia* addressed to Eugene IV, Valla queries whether he did not, in the Dialogue concede too much in admitting that the monastic life, while not *melior,* might be *tutior.* "Etenim via a Christo tradita nulla est tutior, sicut nec melior, in qua nulla professio nobis injungitur." [43] However this may be, the Dialogue is an instance

41 F. Gabotto has an article on L'epicureismo di L. Valla in *Rivista di filosofia scientifica* for 1889 (pp. 651-672).

42 Published by Vahlen—*Laurentii Vallae opuscula tria.* Sitz-ber. Phil. Hist. Classe, Vienna Acad. 1869, B'd 62, pp. 99-134.

43 "There is no safer path, there is no better path than that one which Christ has shown us; and yet no declaration of faith can bind us to that path." Luther took a like position regarding monks' vows. See Vol. II, Chap. 4.

of the cold light of a new worldly reason, without faith, playing upon the monastic argument.

This *Apologia* did not make Rome livable for Valla till after Eugene had been succeeded by that lover of the humanists, Nicholas V. Then indeed Valla might return, to spend the last decade of his life in the city he loved best. Nicholas set him to work translating Thucydides, and other Greek works, it being this Pontiff's darling wish to possess the Greek literature in readable Latin. The huge income from the papal Jubilee of 1450 enabled him to subsidize the scholar world and set it to this task.

Yes, wealth and humanism went together; nor did these flattering humanists care for the glory of a threadbare coat. The *joi de vivre* and a more splendid life suitably accompanied the renewed delight in the classics, themselves exponents of a full round of human quality, and friendly to the glory of this world. Those ancients were nobly garbed and splendid gentlemen; and it will seem proper enough that the elderly and none too prosperous Machiavelli, living on his farm, after coming in from his daily rustic mire, should lay aside his dirty clothes, and put on *abiti regali e curiali,* before sitting down with those stately masters of the world. Moreover, a taste for letters and the love of luxury and art and splendor, naturally are found together in those lordly patrons, those proper amateurs, of the fifteenth and sixteenth centuries in Italy; and craft and letters often would work together in the creation of the work of art, as when Bruni was called in to advise upon the choice of subjects for Ghiberti's doors to the Baptistry.

If the other humanists had been, and were to be, artists in words, Valla was a man of science, whether as philologist or philosopher. His literary powers were not marked, and his instinct was at fault in his weeding out of current Latin usage, and his demand for a no longer possible adherence to the classic phrase and use of words. After all, the question of writing classical or unclassical Latin was becoming a battle of shades, in the face of the likewise academic strife between Latin and the *volgare,* and the actual literary triumph of the latter. One should realize that in Italy the study of the Latin humanities was a phase of human growth, leading on to a fuller expansion and expression of humanity not only in art but in the other living medium, to wit, the *volgare*. The humanists of the fifteenth century were not quite so dumb as to fail to see the worth of the Italian works of Dante, Petrarch and Boccaccio.

Chapter 3

Lorenzo, Poliziano, Ariosto, Tasso

TOUCHING THE EARLIER HUMANISTS spoken of in the last chapter, one may ask, what advance of thought, what growth of human intelligence, what novelties of expression do they present? They drew inspiration from Petrarch and Boccaccio; and more unreservedly than had been possible in the Middle Ages, their minds were fixed upon the intellectual and artistic concerns of mortal life. They were disposed to love it all; only upon intrusive reminders would they doff their caps to the threats and promises of their religion.

Palpably and, as it were, externally, their education and progress hung upon devotion to the antique, its study and its imitation. They brought to the reading of the classics a renewed openness of mind, and perceived their significance more truly than mediaeval students. The early fifteenth century to which they belonged had profited from the increase of wealth and the accumulation of experience. The fields of knowledge were broadening. And if Petrarch was a better classical scholar than anyone before him, he was surpassed by his successors, who availed of his example and accomplishment. Many lost classics had been brought to light by eager searches through forgotten places; and a century of devotion to the classics bore its fruit.

The veritable progress of these men, so far as it existed, lay within themselves, although seemingly it issued from their studies. Those we have taken as examples were diligent and clever; and at least one among them showed an incisively critical intelligence. Yet intelligent and clever as were Valla, Filelfo, Poggio and Bruni, they do not appear to have evolved and compassed novel and interesting modes of expression, which are the sure proof and exponent of human progress. They were still students and assemblers; their self-expression lay in their ardent scholarship. Perfected and, as it were, classical forms of humanistic expression in Latin and Italian prose and verse were to arise from the finished humanistic genius of younger men, who likewise had absorbed the accomplishment of their immediate predecessors.

I

Some of these younger men were notable artist-scholars; one or two of them were extraordinary personalities. Not merely they surpassed their predecessors in knowledge of the classics; they had achieved a more intimate appropriation and transmutation of them into active faculty. They can do more with them, or with the knowledge and discipline acquired through their study. Beyond this, they can do more with the *volgare,* than the men nearer to Petrarch; they have attained, partly through their classic discipline, a better mastery over the proper forms of Italian compositions in prose and verse. They have reached the power to express artistically the fruits of their discipline and knowledge. Like their immediate forbears, they owe much to each other, much to the circumstance that there is an enthusiastic well-equipped group of them. They help each other in their education and their work. More particularly Lorenzo the Magnificent and Politian, whom we especially have in mind, were assisted by one of the last and most admirable of Cosimo's protégés, Ficino, who was born in 1433, and was to be the central luminary of the Platonic Academy in Florence. He will be considered in a future chapter, in connection with the philosophy of the period.

Cosimo's grandson, Lorenzo, merits the epithet of superman, from his qualities of temperament, his exceeding energy, and his notable and diverse powers. He was an Italian of his time. This most astute and unscrupulous politician sang ballads of his own making in the streets of his city, equally to please the people and himself. If he ruled his people, he belonged to them, and delighted in them, in their songs, in their fêtes and dances, and in the hot embraces of their daughters. He was reputed as licentious as he was intellectual. The splendid and unbridled festivals, with which he tamed and debauched the Florentines, gave him spontaneous joy. No mere politician, no merely voracious ruler, but only one who had, besides, another nature, could have written this verse from his *Trionfo di Bacco e Arianna*:

> Quant' è bella giovinezza,
> Chi si fugge tuttavia!
> Chi vuol esser lieto, sia:
> Di doman non c'è certezza.[1]

The lines dance of themselves, as Lorenzo also danced from delight.

Educated in the classics, instructed in some sort of antique philosophy, he still loved his own Italian literature and his Italian tongue. He was a deep admirer of Dante, a devoted lover and imitator of Petrarch's *Canzoniere*. He defended the *volgare,* and with such success, or in such accord with life's insistence to express itself in the vernacular, that the *volgare* needed no advocate after him to maintain its complete supersession of Latin as the vehicle of living literature. Lorenzo gives his voice for the *volgare,* not only because it is in general use, but because it is "copiosa e abondante, ed atta a esprimer bene il senso e il concetto della mente," and because of its "dolcezza ed armonia," and because of its good repute and fame and the many noble things already written in it.[2]

Doubtless Lorenzo's most effective vindication of the

[1] How lovely is youth, which flies away nevertheless! He who wishes to be happy, let him: Of the morrow there's no certainty.

[2] See the great Florentine edition of the *Opere de Lorenzo de' Medici*, Vol. IV, p. 15, sqq.

volgare was his use of it in his ballads and other writings;
—indeed it had already won the victory in the greatest of
all literary creations of the Italian mind and mood, the
Divina Commedia. One might as well realize the essential
feebleness and sheer academic quality of whatever the
humanists had said or done to re-classicize and maintain
the literary vitality of Latin. One will still encounter mis-
prisals of the *volgare*,[3] but they had no effect upon the
period's real progress in thought and faculty.[4]

Cosimo was an able financier and politician, and an intelligent patron of arts and letters. With equal ability in
politics and statecraft, Lorenzo had but casual taste for
banking, and even in politics, with his enormous aptitude,
and under the incessant need to guard his power and life,
he shows the dilettante nature, which is amused by its
task, rather than absorbed in it. Was not Lorenzo entertained by all the means he used to beguile and rule the
Florentines? Must he not have enjoyed that possibly last
cast of the die, when he went to Naples and put himself
within the power of his enemy, King Ferdinand, and won
a favorable peace from him by sheer virtuosity of argument?

Indeed in Lorenzo one has the superman as dilettante,
a character which he shows more clearly in fields other
than politics. A dilettante was he in things spiritual; he
would try the charm of this and that—would turn from
love-songs to Augustine and then again to music. What a
connoisseur he was; and a collector, if not unrivalled, at
least unequalled in Italy; and with what copiousness he
spoke on painting, sculpture, philosophy, poetry and
music! Lavish in his expense, lavish in his patronage of
letters. And yet even as dilettante, he was still the man of

3 For instance, L. Gyraldus, *De Poetis nostrorum temporum,* ed.
by Wotke, (Berlin, 1894), p. 40 and p. 85.

4 Yet such a considerable man as Pontano wrote altogether in
Latin. Although born in Umbria, he was much more of a Neapoli-
tan than a north Italian. See A. Gaspary, *Ges. der italienischen
Literatur,* B'd II, pp. 301-321.

more than human energy, always the superman: whether in his discourses or his revels, or his licentiousness, and so markedly in the mass of his vivid poetry. Political power came to him when he was twenty-one; and he was but forty-four when he died, leaving, as some think, Italy to break in ruin after him for lack of his shrewd balancing mind.

Politian's often quoted letter to one Jacobus Antiquarius describing Lorenzo's pious death, is to be taken rather as a comment on the times than on Lorenzo individually, a comment on the times indeed, that toward the last gasp a famous doctor should arrive with a *medicamentum* compounded of pearls and all manner of gems. It was administered, and still the patient died. After his death, prodigies currently were reported.

A certain Benedetto of Montepulciano, which was in the Florentine territory, realizing that he was in danger of assassination from his wicked neighbors, recommended himself and his children to the protection of Piero, son of Cosimo, and father of Lorenzo, and was murdered some months after, as he had feared. His eldest child, Angelo, was sent to Florence. This was in 1464, when Angelo was ten years old. Apparently he lived and studied in poverty for several years, and attended lectures at the Florentine *Studium Generale* or University, which, having started in 1321, was re-inaugurated in the year of the great pestilence, 1348, according to Matteo Villani.

Probably the Medici knew of Angelo, and of his studying in the School. His precocity attracted the notice of Ficino, and the flowing translation of the second book of the *Iliad* which he sent to Lorenzo in 1470, apparently led Lorenzo himself, so young and newly come to power upon his father's death, to remove the "Homeric youth" from his poor lodgings to a Medici palace. From that time until his death twenty-four years later this Angelo, called Poliziano from his birth place, was praised and fostered as the paragon of poets and scholars. In the minds, or words, of some of his admirers such was the masterful excellence of his translation of those few books of the *Iliad,* that old Homer, but for his natural patriotism, would have wished himself a Latin. Nor has the name of Politian ever lost its glamor; his name and face, and the fame of Lorenzo's friendship for him, still touch the imaginations of men and women who love Florence.

One need not credit the myth of his having produced the *Giostra,* at the age of fourteen. He was over twenty when he composed that piece, and had written the *"Orfeo"* two years before. Soon he began to lecture in the rooms where he had been a learner, and men of twice his age came from near and far to listen to his fluent learning. For Florence it was the very golden time of letters and Platonism,—those short decades which were still to pass before Lorenzo's death in 1492. Then came revulsions and catastrophes. Politian died in 1494, at the age of forty, having seen the approach of evil days; and Ficino died, a much older man, in 1499; while the most astounding phoenix of them all, Pico, prince of Mirandula, had ascended to his star the same year with Politian, when but little over thirty.[5] Savonarola was left to reform the threatened city, and go to the stake in 1498.

Politian was a Greek scholar. He wrote Latin admirably. He excelled as a poet in the *volgare*: the bosom friend of Lorenzo could not pretend to despise the *volgare*. Indeed it triumphed distinctly in this humanist of humanists, in whom, as with Boccaccio, it reaped the benefit of the classical *disciplina*. Politian brought Latin metrical suavity to Italian verse, and his poems became veritably popular, and took root among the people. He also, like Lorenzo, often imitated Petrarch's sonnets. There was not very much originality in his Italian poetry. Yet through his skill, and because he could draw from nature as well as from books, his poems on love and springtime have a delightfulness which is their own.

5 On Pico see Vol. V, Chap. 1.

From his youth, Politian studied and absorbed, and through his life never ceased to assimiliate, the classics. Although he lectured on many parts of the philosophy of Aristotle, and wrote whimsical *Praelectiones* to his courses, he insisted in one of these that he was not a philosopher, but an interpreter, having the equipment of a *grammaticus,* according to the Greek word, or *literatus,* as one should say in Latin: "nec aliud inde mihi nomen postulo quam grammatici." [6] Politian was not a serious Aristotelian; nor was his knowledge of Plato always worthy of a pupil of Ficino; at least he makes an unaccountable slip in this same Praelectio, when he gives the Platonic fable of the shadow-seers in the cave, and ascribes it to Iamblichus, "whom the consensus of Ancient Greece called divinissimum." Altogether this is rather dreadful, seeing that "Ancient Greece" knew nothing of that fourth century hierophant, and we hope would not have regarded him highly. Yet if Politian cultivated Iamblichus more than the veritable Plato, he did but follow the tendency of his time really to read and enjoy the later Greek and Latin authors. His own *Giostra* reeks with Statius and was modelled on those poems of eulogy which, with their mingled elements of myth and lyricism, are to be found in Latin literature from the time of Statius to its last decline. [7]

In the *Orfeo,* Politian did a stroke of genius, by applying the form of the Mystery-representation to the classic fable of Orpheus and Eurydice. He wrote this short and pleasant piece for a festival at the Mantuan Court of the Gonzagas in 1471; a lovely little pastoral play he made of it, a different and lesser *Comus,* less transforming, less transcen-

---

[6] "nor do I request any name for myself other than that of a professor of language." Politian gave the title of "Lamia" to his Praelectio to the course on the *Prior Analytics.* It is printed in Del Lungo's *Florentia* (Florence 1897), pp. 133 sqq. The phrase quoted is from pages 169-170.

[7] Carducci, p. xlviii, of the introduction to his edition of *Le Stanze, l'Orfeo e le Rime* (Florence 1863).

dent, if one will.[8] With the borrowed fable went many borrowings of classical phrase and sentiment quite naturally, and all so trippingly and lightly put together, fused into a melodious idyllic play.

Much the same may be said of the *Stanze per la Giostra,* a more difficult and slowly composed poem, descriptive, rather than dramatic. It was intended to immortalize the prowess of Giuliano de'Medici in the jousts, and his love for the gentle Simonetta, whose death followed not long after. Either that sad event, or the catastrophe of Giuliano's own assassination in 1478, discouraged the completion of a poem which may have proved tiresome to its author. For, as the subject of an elaborate composition, the matter was empty enough, though Politian made the most of

Le gloriose pompe e' fieri ludi,[9]

commanded by the great house who would thus show how they had turned from banking to the noble arts of chivalry. Reading the poem, one can hardly believe one's eyes, and the learned footnotes of Carducci's edition, to find its sonorous octaves built of reminiscence, sentiment and phrase taken from classic poetry; not "taken," perhaps, but rather imbibed, breathed in, appropriated, made the new poet's own, and breathed forth again, or at least re-

---

8 The pastoral composition which was read far and wide, and influenced French and English literature, was the *Arcadia* of the valiant and worthy scholar, the Neapolitan, Sannazaro. The work belongs to the last decade of the fifteenth century. It was a pastoral romance in prose and verse. Its author had Virgil and Theocritus on his tongue's end, and knew the Greek romances. For Italian antecedents, the work harked back perhaps to Boccaccio's *Filocolo* and his *Ameto.* It was the cleverest of mosaics of borrowings and imitations, filled with the sentiments and phrases of the old bucolic poems, which the author used as naturally as if they were the current words of his language. It also incorporated long extracts from those poems. It is edited, with introduction and discussions by Scherillo (Turin, 1888). Tasso's *Aminta* (1573) and Guarini's *Pastor Fido* (1581) are more organic compositions than either the *Arcadia* or the *Orfeo.*

9 The glorious pomp and proud games.

issued, in flowing and well molten verse. Lucretius, Virgil, Ovid, Statius, Claudian, with touches from the Greeks, are there. But in the *Orfeo* and the *Giostra,* as well as in Politian's love poems and ballads, not merely sentiments and phrases were borrowed from the antique; but more subtly the discipline and order of classic letters were drawn into Italian poetry.

So the classical literature yielded forms and phrases to these humanists, through which they gave expression to their tastes and their own natures, though in borrowed or imitated language, and, as it were, at second hand. The spirit of the *Orfeo* and the *Giostra* likewise reflects something of the spirit of the antique, as a summer pool, stirred by a sunny breeze, reflects, with a brightness of its own, the branches waving overhead.

Politian was not satisfied with merely studying, understanding, and enjoying the classics. He would follow and imitate their beauty, reproduce that in words of his own, whether in Latin or Italian. For he and others of his time were endeavoring to transform their knowledge of classic style and substance into a facility of their own in Latin composition. And then they would bring all this disicpline to the aid of their Italian prose and verse. This meant to turn knowledge into art, and, in accordance with the Italian nature, into the art of producing that which was beautiful in form.

But the endeavor to imitate the phrases, and follow the patterns, of classic literature tended to make form the chief consideration, and to disregard substance. Yet these unoriginal composers were not so conscious of their emptiness; nor did they really intend to set mere empty form (were such conceivable) before them as their goal. An endeavor to be and express themselves is observable in the best among them, and, curiously enough, in this paragon of a Politian, who was in fact so unoriginal and for the most part indifferent to substance. More than once he reminded his pupils that their own talents and judgment should not be buried beneath other men's opinions. He also adjured them not to blunt the point of their discourses with overmuch verbosity, nor lose the thread of argument.[10] And again, when someone had said that his own letters were not Ciceronian, he had answered "in epistolari stilo silendum prorsus esse de Cicerone." [11] But if another should accuse him of imitating Cicero, he might answer: "nihil mihi esse magis in votis quam ut vel umbram Ciceronis assequar." [12] So the propriety of following or ignoring Cicero depended on what one was writing; in letters there is a virtue in negligence. He blames his friend Paulus Cortesius, a great stickler for Ciceronian Latinity, for blind imitation: and if it be said: "Thou dost not speak like Cicero—non exprimis Ciceronem—what then! for I am not Cicero. Yet, as I opine, I express myself—me tamen exprimo." [13]

Politian, dead at forty, was also a wonderful scholar; one is tempted to call him an "elegant" scholar, but without using that term disparagingly. His sheer scholarship is shown in his *Miscellanea,* a work of the nature of Valla's *Elegantiae,* and composed of matter from the lectures given at the University. It discussed all sorts of questions affecting scholarship: the origins of classic institutions and ceremonies, the significance of fables, words and their uses, even spellings. His mind was clear and penetrating; his treatment pertinent to the matter; and he showed a true scholarly aversion to pretense and subterfuge. He was an admirable critic and restorer of better readings in corrupt texts. The *Miscellanea* met the needs of an advancing scholarship, just as, some centuries before, the needs of a scantier knowledge were met by orthographies and grammars. Politian was also a valiant translator from the Greek. Besides those early glorious

10 Cf. Del Lungo, *Florentia,* p. 131.

11 "that in writing letters, it is best to say nothing of Cicero."

12 "Nothing is more prominent in my prayers than the wish that I should attain the spirit of Cicero." *Omnia Opera Angeli Politiani* (Venice, Aldus 1498) Ep. 1 to Petrus Medici.

13 In Lib. VIII of epistles, same edition.

translations from the *Iliad,* he rendered into Latin Herodian's *History,* the *Enchiridion* of Epictetus, and the *Problemata* of Alexander Aprodisias.

Whatever a man may say, the truth of him lies in what he does preponderantly. And preponderantly Politian was the ideal Italian humanist, wonderfully clever in his faculty of giving beauty, perhaps a new beauty, to his assimilation of classic sentiments and phrases; not deeply caring for the validity or seriousness of the substance, but beyond others clever in reaching the form which pleases, whatsoever be the content which is therein beautified.[14] Withal one may appreciate his excellent judgment by contrasting the opinions of his young friend who disagreed with him.

Paulus Cortesius, to give his name in Latin form, as he would have preferred, was a younger member of the Florentine group of humanists. He had upbraided Politian for the lack of Ciceronian qualities in his letters, and had been taunted by him for his own ape-like imitative habits. He defended his implicit copying of Cicero, but added that he preferred to be called his *filius* or *alumnus,* rather than his *Simia!* In 1490 he dedicated to Lorenzo a *Dialogus de hominibus doctis,*[15] which spoke (rather rashly) of past and present Florentine notables. To the learned, says he, Dante, Petrarch and Boccaccio are already antiquated. The first is as an old picture with its colors gone, while its lines still please. His poem was wonderful—if he had only put his marvellous thoughts in Latin! As for

---

[14] Francesco de Sanctis calls Politian "la piu spiccata espressione della letteratura in questo secolo. Ci è già l'immagine schietta del letterato, fuori di ogni participazione alla vita publica, vuoto di ogni coscienza religiosa o politica o morale. . . . Il Poliziano aveva uno squisito sentimento della forma nella piena indifferenza di ogni contenuto." From page 367 of *Storia della Letteratura italiana* (Naples, 1870)—whatever else one reads for information, De Sanctis always should be read for his impressive suggestiveness.

[15] Printed in a volume entitled *Philippi Villani liber de civitatis Florentiae famosis civibus etc.,* ed. by G. C. Galletti (Florence 1847).

Petrarch, a man, of course, greatly to be admired, his rough style is scarcely Latin; his matter was composed diligently, rather than elegantly. Naturally the "*ornamenta scribendi* were lacking to a man born *in faece omnium saeculorum.*"

Cortesius then censures Boccaccio's Latin and Coluccio's, which never laid aside *asperitas* and *maestitia.* Bruni was the "first to bring a certain rhythmic tone to that rough way of writing; and he certainly gave us something rather brilliant . . . weighty and judicious in everything, for those times he was not uncultivated." His *History* was better than his funeral orations because "there remained no funeral orations from the ancient authors for him to imitate." One may praise him as learned and eloquent, and the best in his time, "but you know the way of our men to approve of nothing unless it is refined, and elegant and polished and embellished." Incidentally, the Dialogue states that "Latin letters had suffered from the destruction of Greece (i.e. the "fall of Constantinople"), since much was brought by the Greeks to Italy, and our scholars were wont to go to Byzantium for study, as to the home of learning."

II

Among the literary productions of the late fifteenth and early sixteenth centuries, certainly one, perhaps two, and possibly three poems have proved a perennial source of entertainment. They made use of that facile and efficient Italian octave which the latest of the three authors perfected to the admiration of the world, in spite of a fool named Bembo, who advised him, Ariosto, to write the *Orlando Furioso* in Latin! This most delightful of Italian narrative poems was finally finished and revised the year before the author's death in 1533. It had been written in an Italy devastated by the lustful struggles of Spaniards, French and Germans. Boiardo, the noble count of Scandiano, had completed the *Orlando Innamorato* in 1494, ending his glad chivalric poem with a cry of sorrow:—

Mentre che io canto, o Iddio redentore,
Vedo la Italia tutta a ferro e a foco.[16]

And Pulci had finished putting together the matter of *Il Morgante* in 1483, eleven years before the fatal French invasion.

Pulci was a Florentine, belonging to the Medici circle; and as the composition of his poem was suggested by Lucrezia, the mother of Lorenzo, so its successive parts appear to have been recited at Lorenzo's table, presumably before such intimates as Politian and Ficino. If these made an exceedingly clever literary circle, they were not a knightly company; nor was the Medici house either aristocratic or chivalric in its tastes and temper, any more than in its dealings with men and states. Luigi Pulci himself was a genial and comic soul, cast in no heroic mould; and one need not wonder that the martial and adventurous elements in his poem should be outweighed by the more jovial. The heroic note stirs indeed through his recital of the route of Roncevalles; but who could tell that unheroically? The half comic giant Morgante sways the poem, and the lesser but wholly comic and abandoned Margutte. Pulci used the matter of the French *Chansons de Geste,* as it had passed into Italian compositions in prose and verse. He also drew from the popular recitations of the same matter, which delighted the Italian folk of town and country; for the legends of Charlemagne and his paladins had long since won a new home and a new life with the Italian people. Pulci did not turn the heroic to burlesque with satirical intent; but the people's loud laughter pervaded the stuff he drew from, and he was no knightly prude, that he should suppress it. The poem is serious or comic to suit the episode; certain passages show a philosophic knowledge which has led the critics to find in them the hand of the author's friend, the famous Toscanelli. For its frequent classical allusions, one need not think of any special contribution from Politian. Pulci was

[16] While I sing, oh redeeming God, I see all Italy put to the sword and set afire.

scholar enough to supply them, and make Orlando apostrophize his friends already dead upon the field,—O terque, quaterque beati!

The chivalric epic was not to come to its true florescence in Medicean Florence, but around the more castellated and feudal court of the Este at Ferrara. Matteo Boiardo was the honored liegeman of that ducal house, from whom he held the governorships of Modena and of Reggio. The same house was to be the patron, niggardly and exacting as he thought, of Ariosto. Both had proved themselves men of achievement in Latin letters as well as in Italian poetry before setting out upon their great poems. These were to be the chief romantic creations of the time. The knowledge and attainment of the period entered into their composition, palpably appearing in their matter, but more vitally in the disciplined faculties of their authors.

As for antique allusions, personages, episodes, enough of them were taken into these poems, and romanticized by Boiardo, and by Ariosto made utterly his own. Then there was the mediaeval material, and the somewhat dishevelled and fantasticized mediaeval atmosphere. Charlemagne and his paladins, domesticated everywhere in Italy, pressed upon the poets. Those personages were too romantically real and insistent to be passed by, and too popular. They were fictile, plastic, ubiquitous in their gallopings and voyages, unheld by any land, unhindered by sea or mountain; as early as the twelfth century those paladins and their emperor had travelled through the East, encountering strange adventures in Constantinople! Then their stories, their progressively romanticizing chansons, went on along the usual way of mediaeval legend, passing from crusading and feudal war to giants and enchantments and wandering damsels, jousts, sword-encounters, and adventures everywhere occurring for their own delightful sakes. Boiardo and Ariosto were also steeped in the tales of Arthur's Knights, whose curvetting careers never had any real purpose or set aim, beyond the joy of adventure and romantic love. Boiardo first, and following him, Ariosto, wherever the Carolingian cycle had not become sufficiently romantic, could readily introduce Arthurian adventure, Arthurian love and exquisite Arthurian courtesy:

> Amore è quel che dona la vittoria
> E dona ardire al cavaliero armato.[17]

This chivalric love which enveloped Arthur's court, furnished a leading motive in the composition of both the *Innamorato* and the *Furioso*. Boiardo was a leal-hearted gentleman, with whom love and courtesy were moving sentiments. The quiet humor, which was also his, occasionally broadened to laughter in his poem. That had a sufficiently insistent plot. Its whole matter, antique, mediaeval, or invented and well imagined by the poet, was made into an artful epic, congruous in tone and color. Borrowed strains were put together with a new art, and made to live again with a new life.

What that new art was, and whence that new life came, is clearer in the *Orlando Furioso*. This was the last issue of the late antique and mediaeval love-and-adventure motive. It was also a harmony of all its elements, and a perfected work of art. If indeed its plot seems to take up with each new fancy, and wander over the fields of the imagination, it nevertheless passes very happily from field to forest, and over seas and mountains, and even through the entertaining and instructive regions of the moon. Every incident, every inwoven tale, is aptly placed and happily composed. The whole forms an ample canvas of delight; no mosaic either, but a well tempered picture, with values and perspectives, and flooded with the atmosphere of high romance. And what compass and inclusion! Its structure was of mediaeval legend; it carried easily old matter from classic Greece and Rome, from the early Christian ages too; chivalry was there, long since emerged from the dour

[17] Love it is that grants victory. And gives courage to the armed knight.

actuality of feudalism, and moving in a spacious and joyful unreality, such as never was nor could ever be, yet satisfying to the whims of mortal fantasy. This still will hanker for a magic lance to overthrow foes so easily, for a horn to scare armies from their trenches, a ring to make invisible, a hippogriph to carry one to the moon; and for the chances too of draughts from fountains of quick love and rude aversion. Such fantasy would have youth and beauty everywhere, with love and wrath and courtesy, and delicious fighting, best joy of all.

Over all his scenes the poet smiles with an artist's sympathy, and with an irony free from bitterness. There is neither malice nor denunciation in his satire, but sheer fun, as when Michael searches the cloisters through for Silence, quite in vain, and readily finds Discord; or when Astolfo flies to the moon and journeys through it seeking the lost wits of Orlando, finding there most of his own as well! Forever famous stories!

Ariosto wrote his poem in a shattered Italy. How he must have taken refuge in it! It had the truth and validity of art, achieved through constantly revising labors. It was the creation of an untiring genius, which had grasped the virtue of all that his and the preceding Italian generation had been acquiring. That had passed into the strength and temperament and poetic faculty of Ariosto. Touching his subject-matter, how could he, the poet-child of his age, have treated it save with an artist's sympathy and with art's irony? There was in Italy no deep sentiment of chivalric honor, and little loyalty to anything, except the beauty of life and literature and art. The *Furioso* was no fierce epic of crusading faith, or of any faith at all. Its spirit was as the spirit of the time and land, playing with a past of chivalry which had never been Italian, transforming it into a poem. Irony was the means and method of this poet's art. Through it alone could the poem be true to the convictions and lack of convictions of the poet and his time. For the poem was the poet's truth; his aim, to make it fit, delightful, beautiful. Only through gentle plastic irony could he fashion the matter of his subject to the kind of epic which Ariosto in the first quarter of the sixteenth century, under the patronage of the court of Ferrara, could create.

Ariosto died in 1533. Tasso, born eleven years after, closed his unhappy eyes in 1595. But his work had been done years before. He had written his smoothest lyrics; the lovely pastoral drama, the *Aminta,* was given in July, 1573, on a luxurious island in the Po near Ferrara; and the *Gerusalemme liberata* was completed two years later. Ariosto's *Furioso* offered the still surviving truth of artistic execllence. Tasso, with a different temperament, was separated from Ariosto by an altered time. The moment was less favorable for the composition of a romantic epic. Italy, sombre beneath the Spanish pall, trembled before the Inquisition and the terror of the Turk, while dully stiffening her sinews with the revived and sharply defined Catholicism of the Council of Trent. Humane literature was critical, meticulous, empty. But a genius was there and would produce a poem, despite the stifling environment and the ligaments of criticism, which the poet's mind accepted too.

For Tasso was a self-conscious critic, and morbidly deferential to the criticism of others, as well as fearful of offending the Inquisition. But, at least in his young years, he was an unquenchable and incomparable poet. He was gifted with melody of language, and an imagination overflowing with delightful images. Reading had strengthened his mind with the discipline of classic literature, and had enriched it with the wealth of fable. Defining his purpose in his own critical prose, he said that he had set himself the task of composing an epic having its unity in the dominance of a single theme or "action," but diversified by chivalric and romantic episode, and with every incident so organically interwoven that to omit a single one or change its place would ruin all. The poet's blood was warm; he drew breath in the sentiments of love and passion; he delighted in the bewitchments of romance, which art might make convincing. He was a potent and very conscious artist.

The instant peril of the Turk in which the poet lived, gave him his theme, the First Crusade. His chivalric and romantic power rendered the theme in epically splendid verse, and festooned it with enchanting episodes. As conceived and written, the poem told the passions and subtler sentiments of love, and made romance and enchantments live for their own delightful sake. Afterwards compunctions seized the poet, and perhaps fears touching the opinions of Inquisitors. So he bethought him of allegory, which had not been within his first intention. He saved his enchanted woods and gardens, and the molten words uttered in them, by moralizing their significance. He even imagined a concurrent allegory as the spiritual double of his romantic epic.[18] Such invested meaning was not far to seek; for he could draw it from his own deeply moral and religious nature.

So the poem passed through many perils; from the critics to whom Tasso submitted it, from his own morbid fears and the qualms of rather friendly Inquisitors. But it was saved, and was to live for the world in its undestroyed charm and beauty. Too seriously religious for a chivalric romance, too flowering with romantic episode for an epic, it still shaped its variety to the unity of a pervading nobility of statement and an unfailing music of diction. A gentle element of elegy preserved its hardiest episodes from baseness. The result was something as uniquely beautiful in Italian poetry as the *Faerie Queen* in English.

[18] See the "discorso proemiale" to Solerti's critical edition of the *Gerusalemme liberata,* vol. I, pp. 37 sqq., and extracts from Tasso's statements given there.

Chapter 4

Machiavelli and Guicciardini and Their Forerunners

THE DISILLUSIONMENTS and civic deterioration which, to some extent, were both the cause and the result of the stricken state of Italy, could not fail to impress certain scholars who had shared in the renewed and larger intimacy with the classics, which we have been following. Such would naturally consider the fortunes of their cities in the light of their classic reading. Ever since the revival of Justinian's *Digest* in the twelfth century by the Bologna School, imperial and royal statecraft had looked to the principles of the Civil Law; and since the time of Aquinas the *Politics* of Aristotle had become part of the political consciousness of Europe. Why not now apply the lessons of the actual political experience of the ancients, as well as their civic wisdom more formally expressed? So it seemed at least to Niccolo Machiavelli, whose practically instructed yet generalizing genius set itself to draw from Roman history the closer teaching of the actual courses of affairs at Rome, and to deduce from them the imperative logic of facts—the *forza delle cose*. Such lessons and examples of political consequences this Florentine gathered in his *Discourses* upon the histories of Livy, and brought to sharper, but more questionable, expression in his *Prince*.

I

There had been bold, if less instructed, forerunners in the field of political observation and theorizing. The

91

boldest had been Nogaret, a Provençal of heretical extraction; then Pierre Dubois, a Frenchman and international theorist; there had been the Englishman Occam, and the important pair of co-workers, John of Jandun and Marsiglio of Padua.

The relation of the Church to secular government was *par excellence* the political controversy of the Middle Ages. In the course of it, the claims of the Papacy were extended to a universal absolutism, while Emperors and Kings sought to maintain their co-ordinate if not superior authority. Unity was always dear to mediaeval thinking, and thought moved in allegories as readily as in facts. Mankind was conceived as a great organism; from which idea flowed endless allegory. Disputants in the controversy between Pope and Emperor argued from mankind as a mystical body whereof the head was Christ. Should this body have one head or two, the papacy alone, or papacy and Empire? Or could a single head be found above the two in Christ? Thereupon the body-analogy was carried out into the imagined details of physiological function. Curiously enough the most elaborate construction of the allegory comes at last from Nicholas of Cusa, whose life does not fall within the Middle Ages, and whose thoughts presaged much that came to expression in the years following his death.[1]

But the men who seem more like Machiavelli's predecessors cared little for the arguments of allegory; and as against the authority of the Canon Law set up the imperial law of Rome. They were actors or pleaders in two notable political conflicts which marked the passing of mediaeval politics. In the first, the national French monarchy under Philip the Fair broke the power of the universal papal monarchy under Boniface VIII: the second was that noisy battle between the Avignonese Pope, John XXII, and the would-be Emperor, Louis of Bavaria.

It was in 1302 that Philip summoned the States Gen-

[1] Cf. Vol. V, Chap. 1.

eral in order to assure himself that the French nation stood behind him in his struggle with the indomitable and raging octogenarian Boniface. Assured of his subjects, he won the victory through his lawyer ministers, who upheld the royal claims with the authority of the civil law. Among them was Guillaume de Nogaret, learned, astute, and daring beyond the thoughts of others. Armed with a letter of credit and some royal vague authority, Nogaret went with one or two confidential aids to Italy. His purpose was to kidnap the Pope and carry him to Lyons. He enlisted Sciarra Colonna and other desperate characters in the plot, and in September, 1303, made the famous attempt at Anagni, the Pope's natal town, where the aged despot was staying at the papal palace, and was just about to launch against Philip a final bull of excommunication and dethronement. It was never launched. Nogaret and his fellows broke in, seized and insulted and made a prisoner of Boniface. To carry him off to Lyons was absurdly beyond their power, and they were soon fleeing for life; but his authority was broken, and within a fortnight he died in senile rage. Nogaret and the King afterwards forced this pope's successor to anathematize his memory, and free from his excommunications the desecrators of the papacy.[2]

No literal dare-devil like Nogaret, another legist, Pierre Dubois, devised a rather far-off scheme, in which the rights of kings should be exalted, peace assured among Christian peoples, the papacy be put in its right place, and the Holy Land recovered from the infidels. He called his work *De Recuperatione Terre Sancte*.[3] It advocated peace among Christian princes as the first step toward the recov-

[2] The whole story of Nogaret is told with consummate skill by Renan in his contribution to the *Histoire littéraire de la France*, Tome XXVII; republished in *Etudes sur la politique religieuse de Philippe le Bel* (Paris 1899).

[3] Written probably in 1306; edited in *Collection de Textes*, etc., by Langlois (Paris 1891). See also Renan, *Pierre Dubois*, in the same volume with his Nogaret. In his youth, Dubois heard both Acquinas and his Averroist opponent Siger at Paris. He mentions Roger Bacon.

ery of the Holy Land, the nominal object of the book. There should be a council of the princes and the pope, to adjust all differences. Whoever breaks the peace by war with brother Catholics shall be punished by the pope, but not excommunicated, since that is merely to augment the number of damned souls, and is less efficacious than temporal punishments. In the case of disputes between potentates who acknowledge no superior, the Council shall appoint arbitrators to hear and determine.[4]

The work proceeds, devising reforms and remedies for political ills. For example: Since the possession and government of the patrimony of St. Peter has caused so many wars, the pope should hand it over to some secular potentate in return for a fixed charge payable to him in some place he shall select; the revenues of the Cardinals, which are far beyond their needs, should in part be applied to the recovery of the Holy Land; the temporalities of bishops and other secular clergy, as well as of the regular orders, should be turned over to lay management, in return for a suitable fixed income; the celibacy of the clergy is unde-

---

[4] In these days of a League of Peace the passage is of interest: . . . quod concilium statuat arbitros religiosos aut alios eligendos, viros prudentes et expertos ac fideles, qui jurati tres judices prelatos et tres alios pro utraque parte, locupletes, et tales quod sit verisimile ipsos non posse corrumpi amore, odio, timore, concupiscentia, vel alios, qui convenientes in loco ad hoc aptiori, jurati strictissime, datis antequam conveniant articulis petitionum et defensionum singularum, summarie et de plano, rejectis primo superfluis et ineptis, testes et instrumenta recipiant, diligentissime examinent. (Let a council appoint judges from the clergy and others to be sought out; in any event, men who are wise, reliable, and devout. Once they have been sworn in, with three papal judges and three others for each party [the judges from the laity must be such rich and powerful men as cannot be swayed by love, hate, fear, or greed], let them assemble under strictest oath at a place suitable for the litigation. Having been given the pleas of the defense and the prosecution beforehand and having sifted out all superfluous and irrelevant material, let them examine the witnesses and the evidence and let them consider the case with the utmost care.) *De Recup.* § 12. If one of the parties rejects the award the matter may be sent to the Pope.

sirable; schools for the instruction of girls should be established, and the present revenues of the nunneries applied to their support. Dubois did not balk at the thought of tearing down and building anew: "It is scarcely possible to discover anything in this world that will prove good and desirable in every time and place and for all people. So the laws should vary with places, times and people. Many philosophers have taught the expediency of this, and the Lord and Master of all sciences, and of the Holy Fathers and the philosophers, has not feared to proclaim it, since many things which He appointed in the Old Testament He changed in the New." [5]

The victory of Philip and the fatal migration to Avignon marked the beginning of the end of the papacy's spiritual headship of western Europe. Its prestige was impaired forever; legitimate reasons for its universal authority could not continue in a predominantly French city, with no tradition behind it. There was danger lest the papacy become a French appanage. Its revenues decreased, and the means to which the Avignon popes resorted to recruit their finances strengthened the opposition to their claims. The Minorite Order was estranged by a bitter polemic concerning the poverty of Christ and all true Christians. Moreover, the growing force of nationality was inimical to church unity; while the revivified antique conception of the State countered the papal authority in men's minds. There seemed no longer any need for the universal papal tutelage, maintained so usefully through the Middle Ages. The Great Schism which broke out upon the return of Urban VI to Rome, and lasted from 1378 to 1417, was not merely the adventitious and deplorable result of an angry clash of tempers and interests between that intemperate pope and his worldly Cardinals, who were mostly French. It sprang from the stay at Avignon, and from all the forces and conditions which had compelled that sojourn. Indeed as one reflects upon the energies of

[5] *De Recup.* § 48, p. 39 of Langlois' edition; also cited by Renan.

national growth which were to break this pope-dominated Church unity, one comes to view the whole Avignon episode, with the dependence of the popes on France, their hostility to the Empire, their weakness, the Great Schism, and all that it brought forth, as necessitated under peculiarly obvious compulsion.

The conflict which those partisans of France, John XXII (1316-1334), Benedict XII (1334-1342), and Clement VI (1342-1352), waged against the German Empire, under Louis of Bavaria, was a noisy battle. Although Louis's unsteady nature brought upon him disgrace and defeat, victory proved pernicious to the papacy, by aggravating its French bias, and by stiffening its secularization to the detriment of its spiritual authority. The papal victory was a victory only over "the Empire," an idea to which no actual might of arms and loyalty responded. But there were powerful German princes, German cities, and a German people, all becoming alienated from the papacy.

In this last lost battle of "the Empire," the champions of the State set forth arguments which anticipated later thinking. Occam, a fearless scholastic destroyer and initiator, took his stand against the papacy's worldly lordship and the pope's supremacy in matters of the faith. More effective enemies of the papacy were Marsiglio of Padua and John of Jandun. Something is known of each of them. John of Jandun was clever, a learned Aristotelian, and withal a sensitive soul, as appears from his appreciation of the charms of Senlis, where he lived for a time; and then from his vivid sketch of the impression made on his provincial eye by Paris, with its motley streetlife, its overwhelming cathedral—*terribilissima,* and yet such that the soul knows no satiety in gazing—and above all with its glorious university. Paris then, as now, was the city of the mind, as this scholar realized.[6] But with his eye fixed also

6 What is known of John of Jandun (and of his *De Laudibus Parisius*) as well as of Marsiglio, is skillfully put together in Tome XXXIII (1906) of the *Histoire littéraire de la France,* pp. 528-623.

on advancement, he did not refrain from fulsome praise of Charles le Bel, whose deafness to his by no means mute appeal turned John eventually to the service of the German monarch.

This was in 1323, and within a year John had helped his greater friend Marsiglio to achieve that veritable hammer of the papacy, the *Defensor Pacis*. Marsiglio, in quest of emolument and fame, had reached Paris more than ten years before, and had been honored with the post of rector of the University. From a poem by his friend, the Paduan Mussato, he seems to have been trained in medicine and physics, and exceedingly bent on self-advancement. He also made the trip to Avignon, and both he and John obtained favors from John XXII, before they composed their book. There is no means of determining the share of each in the work, though one may surmise that John supplied the Aristotelian learning, and Marsiglio the constructive plan and the envenomed thought that the papacy was in its very nature the chief disturber of that peace of the world which it was the aim of the *Defensor Pacis* to establish. As the decades wore on after their deaths, fame ascribed the leading rôle to Marsiglio.[7]

Divided into three parts, the work sets forth in logical continuity the authors' conception of the State, then their ideas of the Church and its relations to the State, and finally the conclusions from their argument. Peace is society's sovereign boon: the chief disturber is the papacy. The Church should be made into a properly subordinated department or function of the State. This is the burden of the argument of this lengthy book.[8]

[7] As to the critical insight of our authors, the worst that can be said is that neither perceived that the "Donation of Constantine," which they discussed and sought to minimize, was a forgery.

[8] The usual, though unsatisfactory, edition is in Goldast's *De Monarchia*, II, folio 154-312. Some of the points of the argument are as follows; According to Scripture as well as Aristotle, the maker or primary effective cause of law is the people or its duly chosen better part (pars valentior). Def. Pacis I, 12. The people may express its will directly or through representatives; it appoints

A year or two after the composition of the *Defensor Pacis,* its authors presented themselves with their book at the Court of Louis of Bavaria. They were his counsellors during his descent into Italy. His coronation at Rome, where he received from the hands of a Colonna the crown bestowed by the Roman People, his creation of an antipope, and other acts of his in Italy, carried out the principles of the *Defensor Pacis.* Apparently the Emperor made John of Jandun, bishop of Ferrara, and Marsiglio, arch-

---

the executive, that is, the Ruler, and may depose him. The ruler is a part of the greater whole,—*pars principans;* he is bound by the laws, and his government will be best as it best conforms to the will and consent *subditorum suorum.* Marsiglio thought that the whole multitude, because comprising the more intelligent part, was as capable of wise legislation as the intelligent part acting alone. It is for the ruler to appoint and direct all public functionaries according to law. For the preservation of order he should have at his disposal a moderate military force, but not enough to make him a tyrant. Marsiglio advocates an elective monarchy, and his arguments lead on to the final conclusion of Part One, that political disturbances are due to the improper claims and actions of the papacy, striving for control, instead of permitting the Church to subordinate itself to the State of which it is a part. He sets forth the successive papal usurpations. He doubts whether Peter ever was in Rome, and argues that in any case he had no greater authority than the other apostles. The constitution of the papal hierarchy is examined and its secular authority disproved. This is the second part of the *Defensor.* The last part states conclusions: The People are the ultimate human sovereign. They legislate through their chosen representatives; unanimity being an impractical demand, a majority vote is valid; the ruler is the people's executive, answerable to the laws; the priesthood has only spiritual authority; it is subject to human laws; priests and bishops should be chosen by the people; the Church should own nothing, and have the use only of necessities; the primacy of the Popes can properly rest only on the delegation of power by a Council; the Bible is the foundation of the Christian faith, and Councils, not popes, should decide points of doctrine; only the community or the Council can excommunicate; heretics should be punished only when they transgress human laws: no one should be forced in his belief; (Def. Pac. II, 9) men should not be held to the Mosaic law, but only to the precepts of the New Testament. Cf. Riezler, Die literarischen Widersächer der Päpste, p. 225 *sqq.* (Leipsic 1874).

bishop of Milan; but whether they actually enjoyed these princely offices is doubtful. Turmoil and trouble resulted from Louis's Italian expedition, till that weak personage was driven to make his peace with the pope, and vow to punish these heretics, John and Marsiglio. This was in 1336; but John had in fact died long before; and Marsiglio seems to have continued in Louis's service as late as 1342.

The *Defensor Pacis* did not die with its authors. To the popes it was a stumbling block and scandal, worthy of repeated condemnation; while to men who opposed the papacy it remained a store of living arguments. A papal bull of 1377 declared that Wyclif took his heresies from it. Through the Great Schism and the Conciliar movement, men drew on it. Nicholas of Cusa used it in his *De Concordantia Catholica* (1431); Matthew Döring drew from it in his *Confutatio Primatus Papae* (1443). Later still, Luther apparently used it and other Protestant leaders, possibly even Calvin.[9]

II

Marsiglio and these other fourteenth century publicists were students of antiquity and observers of affairs. To them the papacy was an obstacle to the peace and welfare of the world. Keenest of Italian haters of the papacy, Machiavelli also gained his knowledge of politics from his experience of affairs and a constant study of antiquity. The writings of the ancients furnished him with ideas, and suggestions for their expression. With matter from his own genius, he still largely expresses himself through the thoughts of the old writers, and conforms his argument to the events of ancient history. In his dedication of *The Prince,* he presents to Lorenzo, grandson of the Magnificent, this most precious "cognizione delle azioni degli uomini grandi, imparata da me con una lunga sperienza

[9] See James Sullivan in *American Hist. Review,* Vol. II, (1896-97); also *Hist. lit. de la France,* T. XXXIII, p. 622.

delle cose moderne, ed una continova lezione delle antiche."

Born in Florence in 1469, he received the usual education of the son of a respectable family. The first real news of him is from a letter written in his thirtieth year, maintaining the rights of his family to the patronage of a certain church. Savonarola was burned in the piazza on the twenty-third of May, 1498, and soon afterwards, the Republic of Florence, being engaged in the long struggle to reconquer Pisa, employed Machiavelli as secretary to the *Ten*. He was briskly occupied in the Pisan war, as appears by his *Discorso sopra le cose di Pisa*. Next, the Republic sent him with another on a mission to placate the temper of Louis XII of France, ruffled at the lack of progress of the war, in which his mercenary Swiss had played no glorious rôle. Their conduct, apparently, convinced Machiavelli that a State's only sure defense is its own citizen soldiery—if such soldiery would only fight!

He was sent the next year to Duke Valentino, commonly called Cesare Borgia, whose doings were causing anxiety to Florence. After this, in 1502, the people of the Val di Chiana, and more especially the townsfolk of Arezzo, rebelling, this thoughtful secretary sought to apply the lessons of Roman experience, in his paper on *How to treat the rebel peoples of the Val di Chiana*. "Lucius Furius Camillus," he began, "having conquered the rebellious peoples of Latium, entered the Senate and said: I have done what is possible through war; it is now for you, Conscript Fathers, to ensure the quiet of these rebels in the future." And the Senate generously pardoned the conquered, making an exception only "of two cities, one of which they demolished, and in the other replaced the inhabitants with men faithful to Rome." With such an effective policy as this, Machiavelli contrasts the folly of half-measures, especially making the point that while the Florentines had done so much to persecute and anger the people of Arezzo, they had left the city intact, and a source of danger to Florence.

In the latter part of 1502, Machiavelli was again sent to Duke Valentino in the Romagna, to watch his movements and report, a delicate and perilous task. He came to admire this fearless and unscrupulous man, and took many lessons to himself from his acts and bold successes, and at last from his downfall through the unexpected conjunction of two facts, the death of his father, Pope Alexander VI, and his own desperate illness at the time. From these missions, and others to Pope Julius II, Machiavelli gained knowledge of political affairs; and in 1506 and 1507 he realized his darling project of a Florentine citizen militia; but what it would accomplish was still hidden! There were yet more missions before him, to the Emperor Maximilian, and to France; and he was otherwise kept busy in the affairs of the Republic.

Things were confused and violent in Italy; with leagues and breakings of them, as well as fighting, among Imperialists and French, and Pope Julius II, protagonist in the restless strife. Machiavelli proved himself an apt diplomat, appearing at his best in his letters and reports. His acuteness of intellect exceeded his powers of action, and even his skill in devising efficient measures. Like Italy herself, he was a mind, understanding much, seemingly unprejudiced and clear-seeing. His own Florence was involved in politics beyond the control of a rather impotent Republic honey-combed with Medicean influences. The Spaniards were approaching; Prato was sacked, Florence came to terms; she was in fact in the power of the Medici before their palpable restoration. The heads of the house were Cardinal Giovanni (afterwards Pope Leo X) and his brother Giuliano, sons of the Magnificent. As for Machiavelli, if he entertained hopes of a Republic under the Medici, with himself an active official in the same, he was to be disappointed. Just what he did and said in those trying times is not as clear as what was done to him; for in November, 1512, he was stripped of all his offices, constrained in his liberty, and the next year, being in some way compromised by a conspiracy against the Medici, he was imprisoned and examined under torture. He was soon released, but write and speak and flatter as he might, he was not taken into their confidence nor given employment. It was only many years afterwards, in 1526 and 1527, when his life was closing, and the affairs of Italy were hopeless, that Machiavelli, with busy patriotism, again circulated among the men and things he could not influence. Shortly after the sack of Rome, he died broken-hearted over the misfortunes of the land and the realization that his Florence did not desire his services, although the Medici had been again expelled. It was in the intervening years of rustication and straitened inactivity at his villa in the Florentine contado, that this man who never was of great importance in affairs, produced the works which assured him a permanent position among the world's publicists.

From the days of Rome, the quick Italian mind had never been unoccupied with politics. Italian cities were the homes of political discussion, as well as conflict. What politicians were the Medici and many of the Popes! And that great reforming Friar, Savonarola, who looked through shows and shams to sheer reality, which might be clothed for him in the mystic light of holiness, had a shrewd mind for practical measures of government. The constitution adopted by Florence in 1494-5, so largely following the recommendations of Savonarola, was excellent, and his tax reforms became the enduring basis of a system tolerable for centuries. He looked to the Venetian Constitution as a model. Its stability and efficiency had long excited admiration, and were yet to endure for the wonder of centuries.

The Venetian ambassadors were noted for their reports to their government of what they saw and heard in foreign courts. These were veritable sources of political suggestion and enlightenment. Ambassadors or lesser emissaries from other Italian cities made like reports. Machiavelli's were clear and penetrating, but none equalled those which his younger Florentine contemporary, Guicciardini, sent from Spain, or there wrote down for his own and others' information. They contained detailed accounts of the general and particular conditions of that land, its inhabitants and customs, resources and military power. Guicciardini was a matchless observer of the concrete human fact. Machiavelli's observations might be deflected to the constructive uses of his thoughts. While the insight of two men may be equal, they will nevertheless see and treat facts differently when one is interested in their practical bearing and the other treats them as material for intellectual construction. Guicciardini never would have reasoned from the career of Cesare Borgia, as Machiavelli did in *The Prince*. The latter was at his best when analyzing the records of history, and drawing general inferences from them, as in his *Discorsi sopra la prima deca di Tito Livio*.[10]

Machiavelli was not a close professional student, but a constructive thinker. In critical knowledge, he was, for instance, far inferior to Valla, who had noticed some of Livy's inconsistencies, and would not have casually referred to the new city *built by Aeneas,* as Machiavelli did. The latter's mind was not fixed upon such investigations. He accepted Livy implicitly. Yet one will recognize the originality of his analysis of situations and results, and may conclude that it would be hard to find, all things considered, a more interesting consideration of the causes of the greatness of the Roman Republic, than these *Discorsi*. Their view of human nature and its motives may be unsatisfactory, yet none can fail to see the large validity of the author's consideration of the human motives and grounds of action which must be reckoned with by those whose business is with the welfare and stability of states. His method is to establish general principles of action drawn as inductions from the teaching of history, of Roman history above all.

[10] There is an English translation of the *Discorsi* by N. H. Thompson (Kegan Paul Trench & Co., 1883).

The preface notes that in law and medicine, people still follow what the ancients arrived at through experience; but in conducting the affairs of Republics and Kingdoms, the teachings of ancient history are ignored, as if men and their physical surroundings were not still the same. At the beginning of Book I, the author sketches the foundation of states, refers to the creation by Lycurgus of a "mixed government," as tending to ensure stability. Romulus, on the other hand, founded a monarchy; "but that which at Rome the legislator did not provide for, followed through the *forza naturale* of things and through good fortune. The insolence of the King brought a government of consuls and optimates, and the insolence of the last let in the people to a share of power, but without overthrowing either the consuls or the optimates."

Machiavelli drew the substance of these remarks from a translation of Polybius. But he soon develops independently the assumption that all men are bad, and act viciously when not restrained by laws, an idea, close enough to certain mediaeval clerical views touching the origins of secular governments. "Men never do good except through necessity," says Machiavelli. And along this line, he argues that the dissensions between the Senate and the Plebs made the Roman Republic free and powerful; yet his argument indicates that much of this good effect was due to the self-control exercised in the course of these dissensions. Nevertheless he shows that the elimination of these tumults would have impeded Rome's march to greatness, adding the remark that "in all human affairs one evil cannot be abolished without another arising." It is impossible to adjust matters satisfactorily once for all. "Human affairs being in motion, and unable to rest as they are, they must either rise or fall; and necessity leads you to measures to which reason would not have led you."

Machiavelli's purpose in the *Discorsi* was to elicit the working verities of Roman history applicable in the construction of rules of political action for the princes and statesmen of his day. He sought its political rather than moral teaching; and there may have been an intellectual blunder in his not realizing that the "political" and the "moral" are but different sides of the complex of social well-being. Possibly there were inconsistencies in his view of the State and human welfare, attributable to the weakness of his will and purpose,—an individual weakness analogous to the impotence of an Italy equipped with intelligence and knowledge, possessed of physical strength and material resources, and yet crushed by brutal forces from without, which in some way drove on with a will to grasp and get. Machiavelli, without the strength of purpose which unifies a man's thinking, was impelled to seek the rule of action seemingly applying to the case in hand, and valid for all other similar cases. His furthest intellectual end and practical object all in one, was validity, pragmatic truth, *verità effettuale*, the rule that may be acted on successfully. Such a rule must, of course, recognize facts, and the forces of events, the physical logic of a situation. It must be built out of such logic, be a true reflex or recognition of force in action, that is of all the forces making and controlling the situation. Possibly Machiavelli's intellectual pragmatism, which of course took no thought of absolute truth or underlying being, was to find its counterpart in those sixteenth century philosophies and systems of physics, which were substituting force for matter as their fundamental conception.[11] In this way, also, his consideration of politics and the rise and fall of states, had in it something that is represented in all modern thought.

Through the *Discorsi,* through *The Prince* as well, Machiavelli's personal or temperamental convictions affect the logic with which he construes a situation and its necessary consequences. His underlying conviction, readily to be gathered from antiquity, is that the state—*patria,* his Italian heart loves to call it—is of first importance and utterly supreme above all its citizens: its ends, its mere

11 See Vol. V, Chap. 5.

advantage, overrides individual interest and private moral-
ity. Religion, a Church, is well; may even be necessary;
but it should be in all respects subordinate to the *patria,*
and promote its well-being. He is also convinced, or at
least feels, that a republic where men are in some way free
and equal, is better than a kingdom or tyranny. Italy is
the *patria* of his mind; would it were united in patriotism!
The cause of its disunion, of its weakness, of much of its
corruption is, and through the centuries has been, the
papacy.

The essence of Italy's impotence and corruption is the
selfishness of individuals, their lack of corporate patriotism, whereby a citizen forgets private gain and private
hate, and is quick to risk life and fortune for the common
weal. There could be no mutual dependence in an Italy
where there was no common bravery, which is strength.
He had proved again and again that the strength of a land
does not lie in its fortresses, nor in its material resources
and money, with which to hire mercenaries; it lies in the
patriotic valor of its people.[12] Such patriotic valor is good,
since it is the means by which the *patria* attains its ends,
or maintains them. So with great individuals, kindness
and humanity are good qualities, which enable the posses-
sor to attain his ends, just as in the proper place severity
and cruelty may also gain them. And in so far as justice
and the like good qualities attain the ends of the *patria,*

12 See *Discorsi* II, 24. In Chap. 36 of B'k III of the *Discorsi*
Machiavelli speaks of three kinds of armies, the first and best
possessing valor (furore) and discipline (ordine), by which valor
is made firm; the second has valor, like the French, and must win
at the first rush; the third kind has neither valor nor discipline, like
the Italian, and wins only by accident. In his *Arte della Guerra* the
pith of his argument is that the strength of a state lies in the
armed people, fighting chiefly on foot, and to that end military
discipline should be ordained. "It has proved a fatal error in Italy
to have separated the military from the civil life, making of the
former a trade, such as is followed by the mercenary companies.
Thus the soldier becomes violent, threatening, corrupt, and an
enemy to all civil life." From the dedicatory letter to Lorenzo
Strozzi.

they are desirable. It is always a matter of attaining ends. Humanity revolts at the thought that the means, in themselves, are indifferent; yet they stand or fall by their efficacy; by that they must be judged; therein lies their justification; there is no other.

Machiavelli was of his own Italian time, part of its weakness and corruption, of its mind—one of the very best of its minds. But well he knew, both for himself and Italy, how impotent is the intellect without strength of purpose. Lacking that, men are the prey of chance, of fortune: "For when men are weak, Fortune shows herself strong; and because she changes, states and governments change with her; and will continue to change, until someone arise, who, following reverently the example of the ancients, shall so control her, that she shall not have opportunity with every revolution of the sun to display anew the greatness of her power." [13]

A man weak in character may write books of different flavor, as he bends to the matter of his composition and the end in view. In the *Discorsi* Machiavelli would show the rules of action by which a Republic might attain power and maintain it. He will apply his same reasoning to a despot, who, privately viewed, may be an evil man. He too, good or evil, would maintain his rule and aggrandize his power; he too must employ means suited to that end—and again it is the end that justifies.

Moreover, if the end be good, that is, if it embrace the welfare of many people, it will seem to ennoble the means, as the aggrandizement of a tyrannous individual cannot ennoble them. Many of the notorious doctrines of *The Prince* appear in the *Discorsi,* wherein the welfare of the *patria* is made to justify the murderous act: "Where the welfare of the *patria* is at stake, you should not consider whether a measure be just or unjust, merciful or cruel, praiseworthy or ignominious; rather, all else laid aside, you should do what will ensure the safety of the *patria*

[13] *Discorsi*, Bk. II, ch. 30, Thompson's translation.

and maintain its liberty." [14] This may be an indecorous amplification of the old motto—*salus populi suprema lex.* But when the end in view is the strengthening of a tyrant in his tyranny, the evil end will seem to us to aggravate the villainy of the means. So it did not seem to Machiavelli, who looked solely to the efficacy of the means with respect to the end desired by the doer. He admired success and the abilities which win it, and not the least among the latter was the faculty of using relentlessly and logically whatever means were best suited to the end. It is the old worship of ἀρενή, virtus, virtù, which is faculty, or better, superfaculty. Machiavelli admires and somewhat idealizes *Cesare Borgia* as the virtuoso, who unhesitatingly uses any apt means. He would never have been guilty of the fault of Giovanpagolo Baglioni, whose scruples kept him from seizing Julius II in Perugia in 1505 when he had the chance.[15]

There is a chapter on Conspiracies in the *Discorsi*,[16] which is an expansion of passages in *The Prince.* It is a masterly examination of the odds and chances and the psychological phenomena of conspiracies. The employment of men who have already had experience in assassinations, is recommended because even brave men who are used to arms and death under different circumstances, may prove uncertain instruments of assassination. Public sentiment has commonly applauded the tyrannicide. But Machiavelli's professional consideration of the best methods for conspirators would not have been affected by the circumstance that their object was the overthrow of a free government.

In reading *The Prince,* one should beware of thinking of the prince as a mere individual. He is also the symbol of the State he rules; and therefore, as touching the justice or atrocity of his measures, one should remember that the

14 *Discorsi,* III, 41. Passage quoted in Villari's *Machiavelli.*
15 *Dis.* I, 27.
16 *Dis.* III, 6.

principle of *salus populi* applies to him, the sovereign. And at the end of the book, the fading light of Italian patriotism casts its gleam backward over the work of the sinister personality of its protagonist, till one beholds, in hope at least, this ideal Prince as the instrument of Italian strength and unity. The author closes with his grand appeal to the Medici to assume the rôle which some centuries later was fulfilled by the House of Savoy.

Machiavelli's famous work suffers from too much logic and the unqualified application of general principles to human affairs. One may doubt whether it carries as large a consideration of human nature, with its gusts of feeling and its waves of unpredictable conduct, as the *Discorsi*. The latter was the slower fruit of years of thought, and had the unliterary advantage of being more desultory. It is especially clear in *The Prince* that one weakness of Machiavelli's reasoning lies in itself—that it is sheer reasoning, and will not fit the unexpected turns of human life. A writer who sets forth, not what men should do, but how they will necessarily act, may fool himself as readily as one who takes into account the irrational and generous conduct of men struggling for ideals or uplifted by a situation. The author of *The Prince* never could have forseen or imagined that which has been the greatest fact in the experience of our own generation, the mighty awakening of America's enthusiasm and resolve for a war of righteousness and the ideals of man.

It is indeed a general characteristic of Machiavelli that his statements are but half-truths: every statement a half-truth, and usually the dirty side. Possibly no man ever speaks a whole one, since the human mind cannot formulate more than one phase of life at a time. Machiavelli at least might have corrected some of his half-truths from Plato! It is clear that one devilish fallacy pervades his reasoning. He never realizes the evil effect of the evil act upon the doer, be the doer an individual or a government or a partly responsible people. Again to refer to our own time, as modern Germany has shown herself the most

Titanic example of Machiavellianism that the world has seen, so has she calamitously exemplified the specific Machiavellian fallacy which ignores the degeneration entering the nature of the evil-doer.

III

Like Machiavelli, another Florentine, fourteen years his junior, harboured the thought of Italy, and hated the French, the Spaniards, the Germans and the Swiss; but unlike Machiavelli, Francesco Guicciardini brooded and hated without hope. He was no theorist, but the hard-headed man of an Italy politically disillusioned and obviously lacking in those qualities which once had driven the small city by the Tiber on to greatness. Machiavelli had unmasked that Italy in his *Florentine History,* giving the story of those wars in which no warriors fell! Wars that might be entered on without fear, waged without danger, ended without loss—if one had the wit! Such was the war between Florence and Venice, which he narrates in his fifth and sixth books: Duke Filippo Maria Visconti of Milan with Francesco Sforza on the one side, and skillful Piccinino on the other; safe marauding, bloodless battles, till the war ends when the Duke has married his much promised daughter to Sforza, after lies and double dealing, tedious, but curious to relate.

This was before the middle of the fifteenth century; and Machiavelli ends his History with the death of Lorenzo de' Medici in 1492. Guicciardini takes up the tale in his *Storia d'Italia,* beginning with the descent of the French, that dire event of 1494, a year apparently marked by prodigies which the historian does not care to discredit. Charles VIII wavered to the last, ready to abandon the enterprise, when he was caught again by the argument of Cardinal della Rovere (destined to be Pope Julius II) that "fatale instrumento e allora e prime e poi de' mali d'Italia." Besides the excellent artillery of the French, Guicciardini gives further reasons for their military superiority over Italians; the men at arms were subjects of the King, and gentlemen, and paid by his ministers, having the best of horses and arms, and, above all, the sense of honor, with the fair chance of promotion. So their captains, all of noble blood, even barons and lords, and subject to the King, eager to merit his praises, and without other chance of betterment. This was quite different from the Italian armies, in which were peasants and plebs, and subjects of other princes, dependent for pay on their captains, who were rarely the subjects of the cities or princes whom they served, but had interests of their own, with envy and hatred of each other; avaricious, unstable, these captains were the mere *padroni* of their companies.

The *Storia d'Italia* passes on through rapine, villainy, and perfidy, the sack of cities and the ruin of liberty. Years are consumed, till the mingled tide of impotence and wickedness, for want of some brave and able man to stop it, nears the Eternal City, with no barrier except the knavery and poltroonery of Pope Clement VII! Who cared? Who should stop it? So the vile army of Spaniards and German Lutherans presses on for plunder,—fate helping, no one impeding—to the sack of Rome. That was in 1527, and in two or three years there is accord between the royal scoundrels, and Italy is pacified, enslaved as she deserved (Ah! if we all should get our deserts); and abandoned Florence is fighting helplessly for her liberties, till she too is taken in the besieger's net.

Assuredly Guicciardini was the successful Italian diplomat and statesman of his time—successful, that is to say, in his own advancement. He loved Italy and hated the priests, but above all else he loved himself, and was ready to bend his sentiments to serve his purposes. Advantageously born and advantageously married in Florence, he was sent as Ambassador to the king of Spain, at the age of twenty-eight. This was in 1511. After his return, he progressed in favor with the Medici and the popes. In his city he occupied one important position after another. Then, in the service of Leo X, Adrian VI, and Clement

VII, he was governor of various cities, commissary-general, president of the Romagna, and held the rank of lieutenant-general in that papal army which did not prevent the sack of Rome. Nor did he afterwards lack papal employment.

During all the years while he served his papal masters —shall we say "faithfully?"—his own opinions, and such feelings as he had, were as he expressed them in his *Ricordi*:

> "I know none more disgusted than myself by the ambition, the avarice, and the effeminacy of the priests; each of these vices is odious, and ill-fitting those who profess the life which depends on God. . . . Yet my relations with the popes have compelled me to love their grandeur *per il particulare mio*—for the sake of my own interest; and if it were not for this, I should have loved Martin Luther as myself, not for freeing me from the laws of the Christian religion as it is universally interpreted and understood, but to see this troop of scoundrels put in their right place, where they should remain either without vices or without authority." Again: "Three things I wish to see before my death, but doubt, even though I live long, of seeing any one of them:—a well ordered republic in our city; Italy freed from all the barbarians; and the world freed from the tyranny of these vile priests." [17]

Guicciardini passes for a man without illusions—unless to be such be the great delusion! Yet, as with most men, several souls dwelt in his breast; and no single expression reflects his whole nature. He could at least appreciate moral qualities, speaking of his own father as a man of "large judgment, and good conscience, a lover of the welfare of the city and of the poor; nor did he ever do the least wrong to anyone." He even speaks of his own endeavor to keep a good name, and repeats that he had ever loved "la patria." He can consider life "as a Christian, as a

17 *Ricordi politici*, XXVIII and CCXXXVI.

philosopher, as a man of the world."[18] Nevertheless, he appears predominantly as a man of insight and clever faculty, pursuing the interests of his employers, and certainly his own. His thoughts usually discredit or ignore the more general human motives, and place little reliance upon such general principles as Machiavelli constructed from his study of Roman history. To him, Machiavelli was a theorist, with his head wrapt in dreams of what could not come to pass. Guicciardini viewed facts as they were. The contrast between the two appears in his *Considerazione* of Machiavelli's *Discorsi* upon Livy; in which the younger man quickly sees such holes as there might be in the arguments of his friend, pointing out, for instance, the fallacy of regarding the disunion between Patricians and Plebs as the cause of Roman liberty. Sometimes he approves points in the *Discorsi,* but again he finds expositions in them suitable to books and to the imagination, rather than agreeing with the way things actually take place. This critic rightly felt that he had the larger knowledge of affairs. Of course, with Machiavelli, he regarded fraud and violence as praiseworthy or foolish according to circumstances. He was not himself an unqualified admirer of antiquity, thinking it had been over-praised, and that his own time in some respects was preferable. He thought less highly of the Roman civil constitution than of their military system. Machiavelli had laid the ills of Italy, and its disunion, upon the papacy, which had been always so ready to call in the barbarians. Guicciardini points out that the barbarians had begun their invasions in the times of the Roman Empire. It was true that the papacy had hindered Italy from becoming a single State; but it were hard to say whether that was an ill thing or a good. A single republic might have made the name of Italy glorious, but it would have ruined the other Italian states. This view was correct with regard to such Italian republics as these men had known, since their way was to exploit the towns and territories conquered by them, without extending the privileges of their citizenship to the conquered.

The tenor of Guicciardini's opinions may be gathered from his *Storia d'Italia*. But his thoughts are put in nugget-form in his commonplace book, which goes by the name of *Ricordi politici e civili*. There his penetrating consideration of humanity appears, and his distrust of theory. "It is a great mistake to speak of mundane affairs without distinguishing and qualifying, and as it were, by rule; for they all involve distinctions and exceptions due to circumstances, and the same measure will not fit; these variations are not in the books, and discretion must instruct us" (vi). Precedents (esempli) are fallacious guides; since they do not serve us unless they agree in every particular, and the least variation in the case may lead to great variation in effect, and those little differences are so hard to see (cxvii). Still, the same proverbs are found with every people,—for they are born of like experiences (xii). And while it is said that one cannot judge well without knowing all the particulars, nevertheless I have often noticed with people of mediocre judgment, that they do better with only a general knowledge, than when all the particulars are laid before them, through which they are confused, while upon the general idea a good resolution may be based (clv).

"These *Ricordi* are rules such as one may write in a book; but the particular cases, which for various reasons call for other decisions, are difficult to write down save in the *libro della discrezione*" (cclvii). Guicciardini's Italian has been occasionally condensed in the following examples of his sentiments:

If you must insult another, be careful to say what will offend him alone, and not many other people (viii). Do everything to appear good, which helps infinitely; but, as false opinions do not endure, you will hardly succeed in seeming good in the long run, unless you are in truth (xliv). States cannot be ruled according to conscience, for their origins were in violence. The Empire is no exception, and as for the priests, their violence is enforced by spiritual as well as temporal weapons (xlviii). Neutrality in a war between others is a safe policy for that state which is so powerful as to be unconcerned which of the belligerents is victorious. The weak neutral will be the victor's prey. But the worst policy for a neutral is to be drawn through vacillation to a course which his judgment disapproves, and he pleases neither belligerent. This happens more frequently with republics than with despots, because the people are divided, and counsel this and that (lxviii). "I observed while I was Ambassador in Spain, that the Catholic King, Ferdinand of Aragon, when he wished to undertake some new enterprise, or make an important decision, managed so that the Court and people were clamoring for it, before he made known his mind" (lxxvii). Do not start a revolution in the hope of being followed by the people; for the people may show no mind to follow you, and may have ideas quite different from what you think (cxxi). "Who speaks of a *people,* speaks of a fool animal, filled with a thousand errors, a thousand disorders (confusioni), without taste, without joy, without stability" (cxl). No wonder there is ignorance of the things past or remote, when so little is known of the present, or even of what is going on in the same city, where often between the palace and the piazza there is a cloud so dense and a wall so high, that the eye cannot penetrate it—so much the people know of what their rulers do, or of their reasons (cxli).

The same mood, or strain of opinion, is not always represented in these *Ricordi;* slowly and carefully the author says: "He errs who thinks that the success of enterprises turns on their being just or unjust; for one sees the contrary every day; that not the just cause, but prudence, force, and good fortune bring the victory. It is true that in him who has justice with him is born a certain confidence based on the opinion that God gives victory to just undertakings, which makes men keen and obstinate; and sometimes victory springs from such conditions. A just cause may thus help indirectly; it does not help directly" (cxlvii).

But again: "I do not blame fasting, prayer and such like works, which are ordained by the Church or advised by the Friars; but the best of all, in comparison with which the rest are slight affairs, is not to injure another, and to help everyone as you may be able" (clix). Following close upon the last, this excellent sentiment takes one's breath away. In the very next note, the mood is not quite the same. Everyone knows he has to die, and yet lives as if he was to live forever. "I believe this comes because nature wills that we should live as the body requires and the true disposition of this mundane machine; for not wishing us to stay dead and senseless, nature has given us the property of not thinking on death, which if we thought about, the world would be full of sloth and torpor" (clx).

And finally: "It has been truly said that too much religion spoils the world, because it enfeebles the minds, envelops men in a thousand errors, and turns them from many noble and manly undertakings,—nor do I wish through this to disparage the Christian faith."

Chapter 5

Italian Self-Expression in Painting

VOLUBLE AS WERE THE ITALIAN PEOPLE, loving talk and
song, and possessing a melodious language, they were a
seeing, rather than a reading or listening, folk. Their minds
ran to visible images, painted in color. Not only did they
think, they felt in images; which thronged in their emotion as well as in their thought. Leonardo was constant to
the instincts of his race in his impassioned arguments that
painting is a nobler and more potent art than poetry.

All Italians, from the unlettered rustic to the much
lettered prince or condottièro, looked naturally to painted
forms and decorations not merely for their pleasure but
for their ideas. The visualizing faculty, the need of forms
to fill it, was part of their Graeco-Roman heritage of mental habit. Those who were conversant with antique letters,
saw the figures of the old gods and heroes, and the forms
of antique personifications. And all the people, lettered
and unlettered, *saw* the saints and angels, the Virgin,
Christ, and even God Almighty, whom the mightiest of
Italian geniuses painted on the ceiling of the Sistine
Chapel.

Books were for priests and scholars. The people loved
painted forms, appreciated them, and could criticise them
too. Painting was for interior embellishment, and for the
exemplification of the people's faith upon the walls of
churches and over the high altars. For the outside, there
was carving in stone and marble, or better, in the warmer

and more salient tones of bronze. Color was a delight, whether within or without the church or palace or civic structure. No building should lack its raiment, pictorial or sculpturesque, decorative and beautiful, of course; but also illuminative, speaking. The colors, lights and shades, the expressive figures, addressed themselves both to the outer and to the inwardly speaking eye of this Italian people, whose thoughts were forms and images, and rarely disembodied or unclothed themselves in colorless ratiocination. Naturally again, this same people, high and low, delighted in the passing gorgeousness, the living, entrancing figures of civic pageants, or those through which princely despots displayed their power and magnificence.

The Italian passion for the delights of vision might becloud the intelligent appreciation of other factors of expression, which might be equally clever and pleasurable and even more to the point. The Elizabethan drama culminating in Shakespeare was immeasurably greater than the Italian drama of the sixteenth century; it was given naked, with no more setting than the needs of its action positively required. But when a play, whether by Terence or by Ariosto, was given at Urbino, Ferrara, Mantua or Milan, it was an occasion for display. Its trappings, its mechanical contrivances and fantasies, its magnificence of tapestry and painting, not to mention the interjection of scenic masking and dancing, tended to distract attention from the play. All eyes were fastened pleasurably upon the gorgeous pictures that enframed it, and bore such stately and delectable testimony to the wealth and taste of the Magnifico who had set the festival.

The plays themselves might be weakened in their composition by the Italian passion for pictures; their dialogue might become word-painting, as in the *Orfeo* or the *Stanze* of Politian. Though an Ariosto or a Machiavelli might write clever comedy, great drama could no more come into existence in sixteenth century Italy than a great era of painting could arise in Elizabethan England. The achievement in either case sprang from the genius of Italian painters or English playwrights, supported by the enthusiasm of the people.

Springing thus from the demands and appreciations of a people, painting and sculpture utterly surpassed the literature, whether prose or poetry, of the fifteenth and sixteenth centuries in Italy. However scholars and poets might esteem themselves, and grace the tables of the rich, the painters and sculptors, with now and then an architect, were the best men of the period. It was no accident, but due to the nature of the time and people, that Leonardo, Michelangelo and Raphael are the true representatives and indeed the greatest Italians of their era.

Who should rival them? In sheer scholarship the Italians were not destined to equal the energy and insight of the Flemings and the French. Poetry, in its finer modes, was clogged with classical conventions and the weight of antique phrase; it was, moreover, of rather courtly and parasitic growth; it fed or starved at the courts of the Medici or the Gonzagas or the Este. The mightier energies of Italian painting were instructed, but not hampered, by the antique; while a far stronger popular demand supported them along a broader way of growth. And if sculpture carried on the antique tradition more markedly than painting, that tradition was as a guiding form within an organism which was unfolding its own living powers.

Nor until Galileo came, might one look to science for rivals of these great painters, who were sculptors, architects, engineers, as well. The best physical science in the fifteenth and earlier sixteenth centuries still consorted with the arts of construction and design. Alberti and Leonardo proved and glorified this union. While Leonardo lived, no other investigator of the properties of things might touch the hem of Leonardo's cloak.

Among the rulers were men of finesse and subtlety, and one at least, Lorenzo the Magnificent, possessed astounding faculties. The rule of these picturesque despots did not lack gracious elements. The Medici, the Sforzas, the Gonzagas, the house of Este, did much to adorn and render prosperous their states. They were enlightened patrons of the arts, taking pleasure in them and recognizing that it was the political function of the plastic arts to spread the fame and establish the ruler's power in the very eyes of men. Nor were these rulers beyond measure evil. Doubtless they exemplified in their various personalities, and in their methods of aggrandizement and political self-preservation, the principles set out by Machiavelli and the clever Venetian diplomats. Commonly they used even truth but to deceive. Yet it was only in their rather personally directed employment of poison, strangulation, and the dagger, that they seem more vicious than apparently greater men of other times who have directed the destinies of larger states. The largest Machiavellian criminality in all history has gone on through the decades in which we ourselves have lived, and has come to its own in war and overthrow. So with Italian rulers of the fifteenth and sixteenth centuries. They scarcely reached the redeeming goal of stable success and lasting prosperity for their houses and their people. Their policies seem afflicted with some sort of impotence:—were not inspired by an efficient, and potentially self-sacrificing, national sentiment; were too internecine; too deeply affected with the cormorant individualism of the men who devised them. So these men, with all their subtlety and deceit and knowledge, will scarcely impress us as great statesmen who might overtop the greatness of Leonardo and Mantegna, Michelangelo and Raphael.

In considering the origins of Italian painting, it is best not to draw distinctions between substance and form. One may assume that the sculptor, mosaicist, or fresco painter, who worked at his art in the fourth century or the fourteenth possessed the current knowledge of the Christian story: that he was acquainted with the more popular Old Testament incidents, with the life of Christ and the Virgin, and the lives of the Saints, beginning with the Virgin's parents, Joachim and Anna. Yet that which filled and

shaped his work would always be the representation of
these salient incidents in the mosaics, frescoes, or carvings
of earlier artists. Their presentation of the same matter
which it was his task to present gave him at once the form
and method and the theme. In these compositions in stone
and color, the theme or content of the work had no separate existence from the form or method of its presentation.
One and the other made a single whole, coming to him as
a theme expressed, even as his task was to express the
same, possibly with modification or improvement. The
finished execution or expression of the theme had been
given him; and not on the one hand, forms or method or
technique, and on the other the substance of the theme
which he must render. The theme was composed, rendered,
expressed, even in such form of expression as he should
use with such development or improvement as his mind
might aspire to, and his faculties achieve.

The expression of these Christian themes in modes of
painting and sculpture begins in the Catacombs of Rome,
where scenes from the Old Testament and the New are
crudely rendered: Adam and Eve, Noah in the Ark, Moses
smiting the Rock, Daniel among the Lions, and the story
of Jonas. From the New Testament are taken the Adoration of the Magi, the Miracle of the Loaves, the Raising
of Lazarus. Most frequent of all is the figure of Christ as
the Good Shepherd, carrying a sheep, a figure directly
copied from a type of Hermes. There were also mythological figures and decoration taken from the current pagan
painting, and Christian symbols, like the fish, the dove or
the lamb. These frescoes range from the first to the middle
of the fourth century, when the Catacombs ceased to be
used for burial. The style is that of the poorer contemporary pagan work. Practically the same subjects are rendered
in the figures carved in high relief upon the Christian sarcophagi of the fourth and fifth centuries.

The themes will be found to enlarge in the decoration
of the great Christian basilicas erected after the official
conversion of the Empire. Upon their walls the lessons of

the Christian faith were to be set forth, as it were, prophetically in the prefigurative types and incidents of the Old Testament; then, in the miraculous and saving scenes of the life of Christ; and triumphantly in the final victory of the Cross and the visions of the Apocalypse. Mosaic was the chief means through which the Christian artists sought to decorate and glorify the walls of the new-built churches with these impressive Christian themes,—which Christian preaching had made familiar to the people. The selection was not left to the artist, but prescribed by custom or authority. These fourth and fifth century mosaicists followed the traditional conceptions of the scenes and personages which they now sought to depict in stately compositions. The subjects were not limited to the canon of the Old and New Testaments; but were drawn as well from the Old Testament apocrypha and from the apocryphal Gospels. The series grew from century to century until they included the whole story of the Virgin's life and parentage, and many a theme from the great company of angels, saints, and martyrs. Yet tradition and authority guided the compositions. The nave of the church was assigned to scenes from the Old Testament and the earthly life of Christ; while the apse and triumphal arch presented the glory of the apocalypse or a Christ enthroned in majesty.

These compositions were an enormous advance over their childlike beginnings in the Catacombs. Instead of the rudest, they represented the best craftsmanship of the time. The dignity of Rome had entered them; the ceremony of Byzantium is approaching. The leading figures have reached a typical individuality. The subjects are no longer given through crude outline suggestions, but are adequately treated, with a larger historical rendering, and a stricter dogmatism. Yet the effort of the artist seems exhausted in presenting his subject with dignity and correctness. Emotional qualities are lacking.

These stately compositions were to be as type-patterns through the following centuries. They were carried on in countless repetitions, while undergoing modification, deterioration, or development; they might even change with the changing spirit and capacity of later times. Just as the matter of a tale may be retold in sagas, and resung in epic and ballad forms; and yet continue fundamentally the same story, though modified and perhaps made perfect, and imbued with a feeling which its first rude telling scarcely held.

At all events, however the style might change, whatever modification there might be of incidents or figures, whatever increment of feeling might enter, the sacred themes were carried on and delivered from generation to generation of artists in modes of pictorial or sculpturesque expression. In this expression, form and composition and technique blended with theme or substance. Meaning and significance, as well as esthetic value, were held in this blended result, this finished whole.

Style, pattern, composition, and the theme thus embodied and expressed, passed through deterioration or development, and varied change of manner, in the centuries between the fifth and the thirteenth. There was the fundamental Graeco-Roman style, invigorated and re-inspired by Christian energy and the need to express these novel sacred themes. Then followed general deterioration or barbarizing. This was countered by the influence of the developing Byzantine style, making for dignity and balance, but stiffening into a ceremonial manner. The Byzantine style dominates the stately mosaics of Ravenna from the fifth to the eighth century. It had likewise much effect upon the contemporary art at Rome. In the eleventh century, Byzantine artists were brought to Monte Cassino by its Abbot Desiderius; and in the twelfth, in the Norman kingdom of Sicily, the final glories of Byzantine mosaic color and composition made beautiful the churches of Palermo and Cefalù. The remarkable reign of the Emperor Frederic II in the next century effected a great revival of palace and cathedral building in Apulia and Campania, with a clear return to the antique style of sculpture, as in the still surviving portrait-busts executed at Capua to adorn the palace of this admirer of antiquity.[1]

The imitation of the antique, which made the conscious note of the revival of sculpture under Frederic, was but a clearer emphasizing of what had always formed the basis of Italian art. Italy itself was a constant alteration and effacement, with an equally constant renewal, of the Rome of Trajan. The face of the land to-day might still be Roman, had not Italy so industriously preyed upon her antique heritage, constantly rebuilding herself from the old structures. It is the land-wide extension of the story of the lime kilns of the Forum, of the travertine blocks of the Colosseum taken for St. Peter's, of the columns of palaces and temples taken for the naves of churches. Not the devastation of war, but the industrial demolition of the antique buildings, has partially transformed the land. But for this, one might still see the Forum and the Colosseum, and the Appian Way, and the whole land indeed, very much as it was in the days of Constantine.

Allowing for changed purposes, even the mediaeval buildings constructed from such demolitions or from new cut marble, still were as antique as they might be. If the Pisan Cathedral (begun in 1069), with the Baptistry and Leaning Tower, represent some development of a new Romanesque architecture, they also represent renewed skill and replenished resources still following the methods and the forms which Italy never had departed from.

So much for building, antique in modelling and method, Christian merely in purpose. In painting or mosaic and in sculpture, not only did style and method derive from the antique, and constantly hark back to its source; but decorative motives also were antique, and the great mass of subsidiary figures, which in the later times of the fif-

[1] See Emile Bertaux, *L'Art dans l'Italie méridionale,* Tome I. These busts have also been thought real antiques. The Byzantine style tends to Italianize in the mosaics in St. Mark's and the Florence Baptistry.

teenth and sixteenth centuries were to reassert their independent interest, and their right to be depicted and re-expressed for their own sake. A fund of antique motives and figures, allegorical or otherwise, had carried clear across from the pagan era to all times of Christian art— a limitless number of graphic and plastic conceptions of such clarity and distinction that Italian sculpture and painting should never even wish to discard them. As personifications or personal realities they included Sun and Moon and Ocean, the Seasons and the Hours, the Winds and Rivers, Victories and Liberal Arts, the Virtues and the Vices, Sibyls, Muses, Sirens, Psyche, Cupid, Orpheus, not to mention Alexander, Caesar and Trajan; all in patterns and compositions, completed forms of pictorial and plastic expression.

In the time of the great inception of truly Italian sculpture and painting—the time of the Pisani for the one, of Duccio and Giotto for the other—these pervasive pagan elements of expression were made use of as of course. The consciously presented theme was Christian, as suited the pulpits of baptistries and cathedrals, and the resting places for the dead who looked to Christ. Yet though the theme was Christian, the very thought of expressing any religious theme in carved or painted forms was pagan, that is, Graeco-Roman, or indeed Hellenic. Left to themselves, Jewish followers of Jesus, like the ancient Hebrews from whose loins they sprang, would have held pictorial representations of sacred personages as rank idolatry— as the racially kindred sects of Mahometans still hold. It was the Graeco-Roman world that, turning to Christianity, required images of its new faith, just as its habit had always been to worship its gods and goddesses in plastic forms. So the sacred art of the Christian faith is pagan in the original demand for it and in its consequent inception.

Looking at the sculpture of Niccola Pisano (cir. 1206-1280) and his son Giovanni, one may realize what blends of stylistic method and patterning, and what intricacy of cultural and religious sentiment and conception entered their work, to be appropriated by them, and made their own. Niccola accepts the topics of his Christian theme—the Annunciation and the Birth of Christ, the offerings of the Magi, the Crucifixion, the Last Judgment—from his predecessors; their methods and schemes of composition were also part of his equipment. Since apparently he came from Apulia, he may have felt the influence of almost any style used before his day in Italy. Most obviously his own early work, the pulpit of the Pisan Baptistry, (completed by 1260) imitates the relief carvings of certain Roman sarcophagi, which may still be seen in Pisa. Toward the end of his career, as when working with his son upon the pulpit of the Sienna Cathedral, he had progressed toward a freer and more natural manipulation of his figures, and had availed of the lessons of contemporary French Gothic sculpture, as one may plainly see in the figure of the Madonna holding the Child at one of the angles of the Sienna pulpit. His sculpture has become more expressive and more beautiful. The son Giovanni likewise shows the French influence; but his admirable reliefs, as upon his pulpits in Pistoia and in the Pisan Cathedral (finished respectively about 1301 and 1311), mark energetic progress toward a natural beauty in his figures; pointing onward to the beautiful bronze door of Andrea Pisano designed for the baptistry at Florence, and to the painting of Giotto.[2] It was doubtless by reason of the presence of so many antique models, that the progress of sculpture under Niccola Pisano and his son preceded Giotto's grand uplifting of the art of painting: a phenomenon which repeats itself in the next century, when Ghiberti and Donatello are the predecessors of Masaccio, Fra Lippo Lippi and Mantegna.

In the work of these great artists of the thirteenth and

[2] The door was completed and installed by 1336. Giotto, born some thirty years before Andrea, died in 1337. He aided Andrea with counsel. Vasari says that he furnished the designs.

fourteenth centuries is seen the growth of a veritable Italian style, which was progressing through the constant rendering and re-rendering of the same themes, and the modifying and perfecting of them, incited by comparison with former renderings and by contemporary living competition. Each artist who does not merely copy some previous rendering, but makes the theme his own and endeavors to improve the rendering, uses his own imagination, and follows his idea of improvement or perfection. He is thus expressing himself: his work is his self-expression. And when a succession of great artists, Niccola and Giovanni and Andrea, perfects, each of them, the rendering of his master, his work, which is his self-expression, becomes part of a larger self-expression, which may be called that of the race or time or people.

This remains true even when we turn to so great a creator of living and dramatic composition as this tremendous Giotto. He too had accepted from convention and authority, and from his predecessors in pictorial and plastic presentation, the round of sacred topics hitherto expressed. It was not for him to seek beyond this circle for novel subjects. Remaining well within it in his early work in the Arena Chapel at Padua, he re-expressed and again presented the story of the life of the Virgin and the story of the life of Christ, but with a power of living and speaking composition which never had been given them before. Herein certainly was an expression of Giotto's faculties and of his realizations of life and the power of painting to represent it, of his nature in fine, whereof his work was a disclosure, an *actualization* in the old scholastic sense, and assuredly an expression.

Yet providentially—for all things that happen fitly happen providentially—there had been a wonderful life which passed to its apotheosis a generation before Giotto's birth; and this wonderful life of Francis of Assisi, with the religious experience of the generation so stirred by it, supplied this inventive or creative painter with a new series of topics, almost a new gospel story.

Giotto did not have to seek for this; it flooded his consciousness, and insisted upon presentation. It was so telling, so dramatic, and, above all, so pictorial. Painters before Giotto had but feebly rendered its episodes. Now he would take it, transform it somewhat in his potent nature, and give it new dignity and stateliness in frescoes which should present Francis as canonized by the Church and beatified in the adoration of the Italian people.[3] The frescoes which present Francis in allegory and beatification, on the ceiling of the lower Assisi Church; those later ones which gave the great scenes of his life and death, in the Bardi chapel in Santa Croce;—are likewise expressions of Giotto's artistic tastes and faculties and composition, of his supreme artistic balance and self-control; they are a self-expression of the man.

Giotto's career held many elements of progressing greatness. Summing up the past's attainment, it incorporated riches of its own, and altogether was a prefigurement of the culmination of Italian painting in the Cinquecento. It was, first of all, a great advance toward naturalness, toward life. Possibly in the imitative representation of living forms, it hardly equalled the sculpture of Giovanni Pisano, not to mention Andrea. The technique of painting was not abreast of sculpture. But Giotto made a giant stride in composition, a wonderful stride onward toward the representation of life, its action, its aspirations and attainments, its deflections, its constraints and sufferings: and all as exemplified by noble beings in significant situations. In this way his painting follows life, seizes upon telling acts, presents significant groupings, with the figures of the tableau naturally participating. In becoming natural in this large sense, Giotto's compositions have become

---

3 Giotto was no painful biographer or portrait painter. Individualized conscientious portraiture had not yet entered painting. Giotto's St. Francis is idealized, more excellent in physical form and feature, than the early Lives would justify. St. Bonaventura had in like fashion transformed the Legend in his, as it were, official life of Francis.

dramatic and endowed with the power of narrative. Perhaps the story of the Virgin and the story of her Son were never painted as tellingly as Giotto painted them on the walls of the Arena Chapel. Painting and sculpture in Giotto's time had to tell the sacred story which people did not read so readily in books. They should also tell the story truly, rendering its incidents as they occurred. None could be more earnest than Giotto in his endeavor to represent the holy scenes truthfully.

In this dramatic naturalism, this trenchant following of life, nothing is more marked than the advance which has been made in the expression of emotion;—of emotion which, whether expressed or visibly subdued, makes part of every human event. Failure to realize and express this most natural element in the incidents of the Gospel had been the great shortcoming of the frescoes and mosaics which illuminated the walls of Christian basilicas in the fifth century. As the truths of salvation and condemnation were pondered on and lived with from generation to generation, men saw them through a gathering emotion, which, for a while, a decadent and barbarized art could not express. In Italy, with some slight advance in technical skill, the endeavor to express the feeling of these moving scenes appears in the thirteenth century. With Cavallini at Rome,[4] with Cimabue at Assisi, with Niccola and Giovanni Pisano, and then with Giotto, whose frescoes belong to the fourteenth, comes a new capacity to realize the feeling or emotion proper and natural to these scenes, and technical ability to express it.

One may also think that the life of St. Francis had renewed men's religious sentiments, stirred their emotions; and that because of Francis and his legend, sculptors and painters had become more sensitive. At all events an hitherto pictorially unexpressed intensity of

[4] In his mosaics in S. Maria in Trastevere and his frescoes in S. Cecilia in Trastevere executed in the last part of the thirteenth century.

emotion is rendered by Giotto on the walls of the Arena Chapel, culminating in the scenes of the Crucifixion and the Deposition from the Cross. The expression of emotion in the faces and the gestures of the Mother and the disciples and the angelic host is unexampled in previous painting or sculpture. These may have been completed by the year 1306, when Giotto was about forty. His later work, depicting allegorically the glorified St. Francis on the ceiling of the lower church at Assisi, shows a larger balance entering his composition; a balance which is well fitted to the dignity of saintly grief, visibly restrained, shown in the still later fresco of the death of Francis, in the Bardi Chapel in Santa Croce. Although the life and death of this most loving and beloved of saints were the theme of his mature work, Giotto's genius for large and balanced composition and his sense of seemliness control the final self-expression of this painter. In the next generation the combination of feeling and naturalness with composition in the grand style, is carried on by Orcagna, Giotto's greatest and most independent follower. The many other disciples of Giotto, copyists of their master, tend to retrograde in style and composition.

One feels that the tradition of antique sculpture was dominant in the work of Niccola Pisano and his son, and in the work of Andrea. Antique personifications, decorative patterns and the lessons of antique sculpture, either directly or through the Pisani, entered the art of Giotto. The result appears, for example, in the beautiful figure of Hope, draped in antique fashion, which he painted as a Christian virtue on the Arena Chapel. At the same time these sculptors and this great painter were striving for fidelity to nature. These two intentions are not inconsistent, and may promote each other, when the artist is no mere copyist of antique statues or the antique manner; but is more vitally appropriating that antique idealizing fidelity to nature which seeks to ennoble the type by following the pointing of nature's best suggestions.

Since much antique statuary survived, and very little

painting,[5] sculptors were more strongly drawn than painters to follow the antique in the thirteenth and succeeding centuries. Yet from Niccola Pisano to Michelangelo the imitation of the antique by Italian sculptors was usually but part of that idealizing imitation of nature, which likewise characterized the sculpture of the Greeks. There was no such servile copying as might have kept their work from being an expression of their own faculties and tastes, instincts and judgment.

Although the scanty remains of antique painting do not permit a sure comparison, it is probable that the painting of the ancients as an independent art was inferior to their sculpture, which might, however, use color or rich materials like gold and ivory to enhance its beauty. Sculpture had the closer affinity with the Hellenic genius, and would seem to have been more highly prized by the composite Graeco-Roman taste.

The opposite was to prove true of Christian Italy. From the fourth century, mosaic, rather than sculpture, was employed to tell the sacred story, express the Christian faith.[6] Mosaic continued the chief vehicle of expression in the Greek Christian, or Byzantine, art, whether practiced in Constantinople, Sicily or Italy. In Italy, with the revival of civilization, sculpture was the first to blossom in the thirteenth century, and was to continue as a chosen vessel for the self-expression of the Italian genius. Yet painting overtook it, surrounded and enveloped it with quickly budding myriad energies, answering to the universal Italian love of painted forms. And if it was the nature of the Italians to see their ideas, or find them, in forms and images, then painting was the most facile means

[5] Pompeian frescoes had not yet been unearthed.

[6] Was mosaic better adapted than sculpture to give such ample expression of the Christian matter as was demanded? Possibly. Yet where the national genius ran to sculpture rather than painting, sculpture was the chief means employed, as on French Gothic cathedrals; and who shall say that it did not do its office as effectively and as beautifully as mosaic, or fresco painting?

of expressing those pictorial ideas on church walls and palaces. Yet the fact that painting could perform this function more quickly and at less expense than sculpture scarcely explains why painting became, and never ceased to be, the supreme expression of Italy. The Italian genius unfolded itself most completely in painting, found in it scope for the study of human beings and of the circumambient world; found in it scope and satisfaction for its love of the gorgeous and the visibly delightful, and for its love of ideal, harmonious, even formal beauty, by which its continuance of the Greek spirit was made clear.

Notwithstanding this affinity with Greek art and the many lessons which Italian painting drew from it, along with its adoption of antique patterns and figures, the course of Italian painting was one of organic growth, a clear and free self-expression of the Italian people. Painters and those who wrote about them, and the people who delighted in their works, regarded the progress of painting as progress in the imitation or portrayal of nature, until the painters should achieve its perfect rendering in their pictures. This view of the matter, which seems to be the view of Leonardo as well as Vasari, must be taken with all the observations and explanations in which Leonardo enwrapped it, and the qualifications which he made and illustrated in his practice. First of all, the many ways of "imitating" nature should be remembered, and the vast and varied range of the objects of imitation. Beyond the visages and forms of man in infinite variety, "nature" includes animals and trees, herbs, grass and rocks, all the natural objects in a landscape, and such works of man as buildings. To paint all these as they are, it is necessary to observe linear and aerial perspective, and paint, or "imitate," the atmosphere, its light and shade and color, clouds, sunsets, rainbows, darkness, and all the phenomena of the air.

Moreover, in order to imitate these matters truly, which include the facts of human life and the actions of human beings, the "imitation" must embrace congruous grouping and arrangement, composition. And if the painter is to rise to the portrayal of beauty, that is, to the idealizing of the objects of his art, he must have mastered their particular realities, before he can advance to perfection, which is beauty, along the lines of nature's truth. To this end, besides the idealizing choice of types and elements, he must attain to principles of inclusion and exclusion, to the high notes of unity in composition, that he may present his theme consonantly and perfectly, with the fewest possible detractions or distractions. It is in the presentation of forms and colors pleasing to the eye, as well as consonant with the spirit of his theme, that he will be likely to reach principles and realizations of pictorial composition, which will bring his painting into agreement with those modes of Greek art which also had passed onward, through somewhat analogous stages, to a like attainment. For example, when the purpose of a composition is to present a significant event, the interest and action would increase toward the centre of the design, and decline to quietude at the extremities. Leonardo da Vinci never saw the eastern pediment of the Parthenon; but in his Last Supper, in Milan, from the comparative quiescence of the disciple at either end of the table, the eye is led on through the excited action of the other disciples to the contrasted and momentous calm of the Christ at the centre who has spoken. All this presents a spiritual analogy to the pedimental grouping of the figures which set forth the birth of Athene: wherein the action and interest culminate at the centre, and literally slope down to quietude and contemplation in the figures toward the extremities of the triangle.

Leonardo's exhaustive notes, or treatise, upon the study of nature for the purposes of painting indicate what painting as an imitation of nature might signify and include. The complete and perfect imitation of all natural phenomena is inculcated and elaborately illustrated from such penetrating observation of natural appearances as perhaps none other ever made. "Darkness, light, body and color, form and position, distance and nearness, movement and rest,—this little work of mine will be a tissue of these attributes, recording for the painter the rule and method by which his art should imitate all these things, the works of Nature and ornament of the world." [7] So he investigates perspective "the best guide to painting," perspective both linear and aerial; then light and shade and color, the appearance of trees and other natural objects, the proportions and movements of the human figure, and all of this with wonderful care and minuteness, and accompanied with such drawings as may not be found elsewhere. There is no detail so slight as not to be worthy of the painter's study, whether in the muscles of the human body, in the modulations of shadows or of the lustre and transparency of a leaf.[8] It is fundamental in painting that the objects shall stand out, appear in relief, show natural modelling; and that the backgrounds and distances be shown in true perspective. In judging a picture, the first thing to consider is whether the figures have the relief required by their position and the light which falls on them; next the distribution of the figures, and whether they are arranged to meet the needs of the story, and thirdly, whether each is doing its part.[9]

Obviously excellence of grouping, with each feature of the picture performing its function, is part of a truthful imitation of nature, and leads on to that idealizing and ennobling imitation, which selects and combines that which is most beautiful or effective.[10]

At this point one touches Leonardo's virtual qualifications to his general principle of fidelity to nature, qualifications which his own painting tacity exemplified. The painter argues and vies with nature—disputa e gareggia —says he.[11] He will try to improve upon her, excel her

[7] J. P. Richter, *Literary Works of Leonardo da Vinci*, § 23.
[8] Ib. §§ 148 *sqq.*, 363, 365, 423 *sqq.*
[9] Ib. §§ 17, 554.
[10] See e.g. Ib. §§ 587, 588, 592, 593.
[11] Ib. § 662.

if he can, in his endeavor to paint what is significant, noble, and beautiful. This Leonardo did, and Raphael, and Michelangelo, and Titian. In order to make his painting effective, the painter will even, literally and meticulously speaking, falsify nature, by altering or omitting such details of appearance as actually may be seen in nature, but which blunt the effectiveness of his painting, obscure the form or contour of his conception or of the chief objects by which he designs to present it. Leonardo says this substantially; and this he also did, and Raphael and Michelangelo and Titian.

Nevertheless that the principle of fidelity, or the higher fidelity, to nature must in general obtain, Leonardo shows in a pregnant paragraph upon the course of Italian painting: The painter's work will have little merit if he merely copies another artist; but only if he studies from nature. The painters after the Romans imitated each other, and art declined. "Then came Giotto the Florentine who was not content to imitate the works of his master Cimabue . . . but began to draw on the rocks the actions of the goats he kept." He drew all the animals in the country till after much study he surpassed the masters of his time and of many centuries before him. After him, art declined again by copying what had been done, until Masaccio, a Florentine, "showed by his perfect work how those who take any guide but nature, mistress of masters, weary themselves in vain." [12]

So Leonardo brings us to this remarkable Masaccio, who looked into the face of nature and saw more perfectly than anyone before him how painting should imitate. Vasari says that he painted things as they are, and was the first to make his figures stand firmly on their feet. He individualized his people, making them look real; and greatly improved his perspective, giving his pictures atmospheric depth. Every figure has its place where there is room for it, not merely for the part which shows, but

[12] Ib. § 660.

for the rest of the figure remaining invisible behind another form. Light and shadow have become important in his painting, as they are in every actual scene. So this young genius expressed his understanding of the face of nature, and died, not much over twenty-seven, about the year 1428, leaving those frescoes in the Carmine at Florence to be studied by all Italian painters of his own time and long after him.

Masaccio marks a stage in the progress of painting toward that complete and perfect modelling which Leonardo held to be the "soul of painting," and exemplified in his Mona Lisa. After Masaccio, or in his time, others worked diligently, bringing out their understanding of how things looked, and endeavoring to arrange and paint them beautifully, decoratively; sometimes raising their types, and even trying to educe the soul. Such a one was Fra Angelico, born before Masaccio and long outliving him. Of a truth he was a saintly soul, and one whose constant study and subtle skill invested with loveliness and saintliness the forms he painted. All his long life (1387-1455) he observed and studied. Starting from idyllic sweetness, he progressed year by year, improving the shading of his backgrounds, thus beautifying them with truth. He raises the ordered composition of his pictures, as in the Uffizi *Coronation of the Virgin* and the *Last Judgment* in the Academy at Florence. He advances in the individualizing of figures and the rendering of expression, and in the naturalness of his grouping, even reaching that impressive and beautifully composed grouping which may still harmonize with the natural. Having impressed the walls of his Convent, San Marco, with an intensive and hitherto unpainted saintliness, he put his very last pictorial attainment into the Preaching of St. Stephen and the Saint's Martyrdom, in Pope Nicholas's Chapel in the Vatican.[13] Thus through his art, and as it were progressively, Fra

13 See generally Langton Douglas, *Fra Angelico* (London, 1900).

Angelico expresses his own lovely nature, which was a painter's also, and imbued with the instinct of beauty and the passion to see and paint appearances.

After Masaccio, in Florence, a realistic and more analytical study of things went on with Paolo Uccello and the Pollajuoli. Then painting turns toward a full expression of the vivid life of Florence in the quattrocento, which shall be painted in its whole pageantry and individual delightfulness. Upon this alluring actuality of street life about him, as well as upon Masaccio's frescoes, is turned the gifted though over-greedy eye of the Carmelite, Fra Lippo Lippi. He is delightful in his cheerful human rendering of sacred themes; a portrait painter always, yet executing many lovely altar pieces filled with pleasing women, he approached great composition in his decoration of the Prato Duomo, even attaining it, and with a more refined beauty, in the *Annunciation* in the Duomo at Spoleto. A little younger than Fra Lippo, was Benozzo Gozzoli, who put life's cheerful pageantry into the anything but sacred scenes of the Riccardi chapel. Still younger were Ghirlandajo and Botticelli. Both were students of Fra Lippo as well as of Masaccio's frescoes, and both were to become famous and significant painters. No painter has rendered on so ample a scale the complete life of quattrocento Florence as Ghirlandajo (1449-1498), a man of extraordinary aptness and facility in composition, who, with his pupils, covered a goodly acreage of surface, and sometimes with admirable pictures. His *Calling of Peter and Andrew* on the wall of the Sistine Chapel is scarcely surpassed by any of those compositions over which arches Michelangelo's ceiling. His best known, and most amply illustrative work fills the choir of S. Maria Novella. Among those quite delightful pictures, *The Birth of the Virgin* excels in deftness of general composition and in the beauty of the figures. Yet Ghirlandajo's pleasing rendering of the detail and incident of life, which made him a great painter of *genre,* scantily covers the incongruity between his gaiety and the sacred themes. In spite of his cheerful attractiveness, the thoughtful mind may be disturbed by a certain pervasive irrationality, or at least by the incomplete rationalizing of his composition. He does not object to irrelevancy of detail and corner incident, an irrelevancy which will serve as contrast to the more strictly drawn principles of composition and mightier harmony of design already showing in Leonardo, and to attain more obvious splendor in Raphael. Yet Ghirlandajo offers a brilliant expression of himself and of his quattrocento Florence.

A very different painter and human being was Sandro Botticelli (1444-1510), to whom Ghirlandajo's successful and rather superficial art may have been a spiritual thorn. Yet he was a cheerful soul, beneath his rather sad and pregnant painting. The charmed study of the classics, pervading a Florence ruled by Lorenzo dei Medici, and by Politian in the humanities, affected Botticelli as a new and high romance. He was touched by the joyful-sad vibrations of their poetry, by Politian's *Orfeo* and his "Ben venga Maggio," and why not by Lorenzo's "Triumph of Bacchus and Ariadne," beginning:

> Quant' é bella giovinezza,
> Che si fugge tuttavia.[14]

His later life was as deeply moved by the strident eloquence, and then the fate, of Savonarola. Yet Botticelli, in some saddened sense, remained Botticelli, and still felt and thought either in allegories or in images which were living symbols. His *Judith* seems as much a symbol as his *Fortezza*. Pallas crushing the Centaur, but not with physical force, whether it signified Lorenzo's victory over the Pazzi (1478), at least symbolized much that then was pressing to expression in the painter's phantasy. A puzzled sense of life's loveliness and pathos speaks unspoken from the face and form of Venus—newly born? one doubts it. The *Spring* is sheer allegory, classical in its provenance, romantic in its quality; and the *Calumny* is allegory so

14 How lovely is youth, which flies away nevertheless!

completely veiled that men have felt impelled to link it with the unjust destruction of Savonarola. But Botticelli was a splendid draughtsman too, having early learned his lesson from Antonio Pollajuolo; and he showed the resources of his composition in those scenes from the life of Moses, painted by him in the Sistine Chapel. Leonardo reproved him for belittling landscape, and thinking it a thing that might be done offhand. Botticelli did not set himself to that as he did to his Madonnas, and to his boys or angels, and to his Venus which allures as through some subtler sense-fascination working within the veil of flesh. His phantasy which pervades his apprehension of the antique, his very personal imagination and indwelling mood, find expression in these forms through this painter's mastery of a significant and speaking line.

A different reflection of the antique was brought to masterful expression in the painting of another man, Mantegna (1430-1506), the Paduan who worked so long at Mantua. His painting drew lessons from the sculpture of Donatello who came to Padua in 1443, and executed his equestrian statue of Gattamalata. This universal Donatello was a gluttonous observer of nature, and here Mantegna gained from him; but the antique had not failed to work upon the sculptor and his fellows: Alberti says that "the spirit of the ancients passed into the frames of Ghiberti, Brunelleschi, Donatello and Masaccio, and fitted them for the most honorable enterprises." [15]

Mantegna absorbed the plastic qualities of Donatello and of the antique sculpture, showing them even in his early frescoes in the Eremitani chapel in Padua, executed before he went in 1459 to serve the Gonzagas at Mantua. He could paint action naturally, and was a great portrayer of individualities when the task was set him, for example, to paint Lodovico Gonzaga and his family. But he had always been, and more and more became a student of ancient monuments and a signal lover of the antique and

[15] Quoted by Crowe and Cavalcaselle.

its qualities. No painter before him had so masterfully brought the lines and motives and emblems of antique art into effective union with his own, one might say, classic genius. He is the great quattrocento painter who advances to that beauty which rises above the charms of the individual and above the so humanly attractive painting which delights in them. Mantegna rises above such actual or imagined portraiture, as Leonardo will rise, and Raphael and Michelangelo. He has likewise made his own advances toward their greater art in the high unity of his composition and the discarding of distracting incident. Such classic self-expression of Mantegna may be seen in the historical composition of the *Triumph of Caesar,* what there is left of it, in Hampton Court, and in the mythological *Parnassus* in the Louvre.

Art is the best criticism of art; and never was so great criticism passed on the previous manner and achievement of painting as that contained in the work of those three great men whose names have just been set together. Two of them (not Raphael, who was altogether a painter) were capable of criticism in words; a more final judgment lay in their painting, and the manner in which it lifted itself above much that had been and still was popular. So lofty and so ideal became the painting and sculpture of these three great artists and certain of their fellows, that it indirectly compels attention to the character of the society in which they had their being, and the effect of it in promoting or hindering their attainment.

There are different phases of personality within that mysterious form which cloaks a so-called individual—as may be seen, outside of Italy, amply illustrated in many an English Elizabethan. The same is true of a people, or of what we call the genius of a race. If its phases are indeed parts of an unity, at least they appear separable and distinct one from another. The virtues of mind and disposition, all the positive and exemplary elements of human being, rarely work together either in an individual or a people. Some of them may exist in marked degree, while others, which might seem their normal concomitants, are as noticeably wanting. One might ideally hope to find intellectual power accompanying a correspondingly large benevolence; one might expect the religious sense of reverence and dependence on the divine to be associated with the social virtues, for which it sometimes is a substitute; and still more reasonably might one look for a close association between beauty of character and a delight in the beauty of visible things and their representations. But we know that these wished for conjunctions fail quite as often as they greet us in the records.

The universal Italian delight in all the delightful things of form and color which may be created, fashioned, or put together by human craft, bore slight relationship to civic virtue. It was connected with Italian religious feeling, because that demanded images, delighted in them, functioned by means of them. It was akin to the Italian critical sense, or reason, in so far as that employed itself upon the pleasure-giving qualities of the products of human art.

Another point of comparison: in a large way Elizabethan plays accorded with the popular taste and the approvals and disapprovals issuing from the English mind and character. But many of the plays, especially those which were *Italianate*, did not represent the ethics of the audience. The audience, listening to Webster's *White Devil* or *Duchess of Malfey*, might enjoy upon the stage what it neither was nor approved of. Likewise Italian painting assuredly corresponded with Italian taste, and yet its themes and the beauty and loveliness of their presentation might bear no obvious resemblance to the characters of the men who ordered the paintings and took pleasure in them. These paintings were what they liked, agreeing with their tastes rather than their morals. Pietro Aretino (1492-1557), the blackmailing litterateur who plied his vile trade from the tolerant security of Venice, was an intimate of Titian and an excellent critic of painting; he was very sensitive to the beauties of Venetian sunsets, and could describe them charmingly.

Nor were Italian paintings necessarily a reflection of the moral natures of the painters themselves. One may fall back on the Aristotelian-scholastic thought, as given by Aquinas: Ars est recta ratio factibilium—the right reason, or way, of making things that are makeable. In itself *ars* is innocent—the *locus innocentiae*—in the sense that the making of a thing, the building of a house or the painting of a picture, is not an act of ethical import; is neither moral nor immoral, righteous or wicked.

It was not the moral natures of the Italians, or their truthfulness, their civic loyalty and patriotism (which were conspicuously lacking) that painted their beautiful pictures. It was Italian love and genius for painting. The genius, the heaven bestowed grace of form, was theirs. They succeeded more splendidly in painting than in their poetry and belles lettres, where form seems won at the expense of substance. Indeed in their writing, form stands out plastically. In Castiglione's famous book, the qualities, the equipment, the manners of a perfect Courtier appear as forms visible and pleasing to the eye.

Painting and sculpture naturally change their style and manner, and incidentally their aims, as they move on to a culmination. The painters of the quattrocento had shown individual differences in conception, method, and achievement, according to their faculties and temperaments. Their painting had been an expression of themselves, and withal an image of the tastes and fancies of the time. Italy had been growing richer; had been constantly increasing the assets of her civilization. There was ampler means to indulge the taste for painting and remunerate the painters. Little had occurred to check life's happy effervescence. The last decade of the century opened as a glad climacteric, at Florence especially; but was to end in perturbation. Lorenzo dei Medici died in 1492, and his great scholars soon followed him to the tomb. The French invasion came, with its easy overthrow of states, to demon-

strate insultingly Italian weaknesses. With their Medici
for the time expelled, the Florentines, scared by the demon-
strations of Savonarola, rather calamitously abandoned
art for goodness; then they burned the prophet, as they
had burned their finery, and returned to earth and art. In
Milan quite as rude events took place a little later, and the
Moro (Lodovico Sforza) passed to a dungeon at Loches,
with the shame of Italy's invasion on his head. Cesare
Borgia too, after his baleful meteor course, had flitted to
a prison in Spain. Such object lessons might damp the
Italian mood. Perhaps sobering Spanish manners were
entering the high society, which possibly looked for a more
sedate decoration of its habitation. Perhaps some influence
flowed from the new study of Plato.

It is hard to bring such events or changes, local or general, to bear upon the progress and mounting style of
Italian painting. Rather, we see the advance taking to itself
the previous attainment, and as from its *milieu* rising to its
culmination. It even re-asserts its affinity with the earlier
achievements of Giotto and of Masaccio, which Leonardo
recognized as epoch-making. But most assuredly this
supreme advance was due to the genius of three men, and
to the significant work of contemporary craftsmen. The
careers of these three began, indeed that of Leonardo
reached its meridian, in the quattrocento. Born in 1452,
Leonardo's *Last Supper* was painted before the century
closed. Michelangelo, born in 1475, passed the susceptible
and pregnant years of youth at work among the art treasures of Lorenzo, associating with his great Platonists,
before Lorenzo died in 1492. Raphael was born in 1483;
he also had much to learn before the sixteenth century
ushered in his eighteenth year. His feet were planted in
the quattrocento; schooled in its art, he took its lessons
with him even to his fresco-painting in the Vatican.

The creations of these men of genius—their self-expression—can neither be detached from their enabling
antecedents nor accounted for by them. Their work passed
onward from what had been done; it asserted its affinity

with what was most significant in the past: at the same time it was distinct creation. Their art opened new depths of truthfulness in the modeling of natural objects invested with the verities of light and shadow. Their genius realized the beauty and the profound representative significance of the human form, which their art rendered with intrinsic dignity and lofty graciousness. They intensified the import of its movements and postures. They grouped human forms and other matter of their compositions beautifully, so as to give pleasure to the eye, and functionally, so as to contribute to the action of the piece. They avoided irrelevance and distraction, and kept all things true to the master motive of their composition.

The mind of Leonardo, analytic, curious as to all things visible and their effective relationships, the mind to which there was nothing negligible or unimportant; the eye to which likewise there was nothing insignificant or unimpressive, an eye that discerned more subtleties in the appearance of things than ever had been imagined; the artist temper delighting in the import and beauty of appearances, eager to fix their fleeting loveliness; the deft finesse of hand which could execute, change, or retract whatever might be supplied by eye or mind; and then the re-composing, intensifying, creative faculty which could present the inclusive and enduring verities of the human personality, and the moment of supreme import in the human drama—such may have been the qualities of this, in all respects wonderful, Leonardo, through which he brought painting to a perfection never before realized, and in its intimate intent and execution not to be surpassed.

Leonardo was a true Italian, to whom vision, the function of the corporeal eye, the sense of sight, was the chief purveyor both of pleasure and of knowledge of the world. Under its instigation worked the investigating, re-producing and constructive hand; both eye and hand reporting the data of their visual and tactile inquiry to the common sense which dwells behind the other senses, and judges and compares the testimony of its five instruments.[16] Painting is the means and art *par excellence* which captures and preserves the phenomena of the visible world—le opere di natura—for future pleasure and enlightenment, and presents them as they are in reality.

"He who disparages painting, the sole imitator of all the visible works of nature, of a surety disparages a subtle invention, which with philosophy and subtle speculation, considers all the qualities of forms, backgrounds and settings (arie e siti), plants, animals, herbs and flowers, which are enveloped in shadow and light. And truly this is the science and legitimate daughter of nature, because painting is born from Nature. Or, more correctly, we should call it Nature's grandchild, because all visible things have been born from Nature, from which things born from Nature painting is born. So we rightly call it grandchild of nature and kin to God." [17]

But the painter is no sheer copyist, for he argues and vies with nature. He shall even have a conception in his imagination, an idea, a composition, and bring out its design, and build it up so that it may express his idea; but with all his figures drawn and placed in true perspective, and executed according to reason and natural effects.[18]

Such statements indicate why painting was one of Leonardo's dominant passions, and through what courses of reasoning he justified his profound interest in it, con-

---

16. . . . l'occhio riceve le spezie overo similitudini delli obbietti, e dàlli alla imprensiva, e da essa imprensiva al senso commune, e li é giudicata. (. . . the eye receives the details or semblances of the objects, and conveys them to the perceptions which in turn passes them on to the common sense, where they are judged.) E. Solmi, *Leonardo-Frammenti* (Florence, Barbera, 1904) p. 241. L'occhio, che si dice finestra dell'anima, è la principale via, donde il comune senso può più copiosamente e magnificamente considerare le infinite opere di natura. (The eye, which is called the window of the soul, is the principal way from which the common sense can most copiously and magnificently consider the infinite works of Nature.) ib. p. 235.

17 Solmi, *Leonardo* o. c. p. 276.

18 Solmi, o. c. p. 278.

necting it with other branches of his scientific inquiry into the kinetic values and relationships of things.

It was impossible that Leonardo should not have set painting above the descriptions and narrations of poetry, being an Italian man to whom all things addressed themselves in images,—to the eye and tactile hand, rather than in words. He constantly emphasizes the greater power, directness, and instantaneity of the impressions of sight, as compared with the infiltration of the meaning of words through the ear to the *senso commune*. Painting presents the essence of its matter in a single instant, and all at once gives the impression of the natural objects in the harmony and proportion of the parts and the whole which they compose.[19]

Leonardo follows again the genius of his people in judging painting to be superior to sculpture;—through its "larger mental discourse," and more universal powers of representation; through its means of linear and aerial perspective and power of bringing the remote and the near into the same composition; and because of its beauty of color and its marvels of *nuance* and *finesse*.[20]

His own painting and his own work in sculpture never satisfied Leonardo's passion for fidelity to nature and for the effective presentation of the modifying conception in his mind. His love of beauty might omit distracting incidents in order to enhance the impressiveness of the painted reality. He had always realized that the truthful apprehension and representation of the outward appearance of an object depends upon knowledge of its inner structure and organic *rationale,* whether the object be living or inanimate. Never did his mind cease to impel his eye and hand to the investigation of the structure of casual relationships which produced the outer appearance. If he was a painter, he was just as integrally a man of science, and indeed one whose curiosity and passion for knowledge

19 Solmi, o. c. pp. 233-251.
20 Solmi, o. c. pp. 289-297.

constantly checked the painter's productivity. In the end, the man of science mastered the artist.[21] The painting and the sculpture of Leonardo da Vinci were but a partial self-expression of this man of insatiable intellectual curiosity and utterly astounding intellectual insight.

Leonardo, painter and man of science, lived in a world of nature's works (which include man), as well as in his own modifying conceptions of these natural creations. But he who is not half withdrawn from his art through following after knowledge infinite, and is altogether painter, may build a world more completely in accord with his creative sense of beauty and other factors of his plastic genius. There had been a Giotto world, made of personages whom we quickly recognize as belonging to it. There was a Fra Angelico world of blessed saints:—who would have the heart to exile a single one even of his somewhat less blessed damned to any region of hard actuality! There was a cheerful human world of Fra Filippo, another more daintily fashionable of Ghirlandajo, and a strange world of Botticelli. There was a world of Perugino, with its admirably composed array of regularly beautiful balanced figures, where one might feel scanted of spiritual or vital sustenance. And now there was to be a world of Raphael, indeed, more than one of them. First an idyllic world like Perugino's, only with a bit more soul; then a world of perfect groupings, mother and child and often the young John, the world of altogether lovely Granduca and Del Sedia Madonnas and Belles Jardinières; and then a finally ennobled world, composed and patterned in beauty, and peopled with beings perfected in new grace. Compared with these final compositions, those of other painters seemed to lack life's complete harmony; in the presence of the beings who filled them, the figures of previous painters might seem to lack something of the fullness of life's comeliness. This world had no meticulous realistic insistences, as that all things in it should submit to compass

21 See Vol. V, Chap. 2.

and yard stick. In that great cartoon of the *Miraculous Draught of Fishes,* had the two boats been drawn large enough to hold the Apostolic fishers, the dramatic greatness of these human figures would have been sacrificed. Yet such was the visual validity and appeal of this final pictorial world of Raphael that it carried no suggestion of unreality. Raphael's historical personages in their portraits, a Julius II, a Castiglione, fit into this same world.

Perhaps nothing lent more beauty to this final world of Raphael than the position of each figure in it: the pleasing relative position as well as posture of every figure in the *School of Athens,* for example. That was part of the nobility of the whole design, the visual effect. The eye draws as great pleasure from the whole picture as from the beautiful figures that fill it so adequately, and neither crowd nor impede or jar upon each other. Thus Raphael's supreme faculty of pictorial composition found expression, and the efficient harmonies of his nature. He felt no craving for novelty; his painting sought no drastic innovation. He accepted his subjects easily, as from tradition. He presents them with more potent and more beautiful unison of composition than had been reached before. Even the so beautiful and so telling contrast of gesture between the arm of Plato pointing aloft in the *School of Athens,* and that of Aristotle horizontally covering the field of nature's works, was traditional in literature, though it might never have been so shown in fresco.

In Raphael artistic interest and creative faculty direct themselves to this perfected unison of composition, this harmony of lovely forms, which admits neither discord nor irrelevance. He conceives the composition as a whole throughout its parts; he represents it as a whole, and as a whole will the spectator see it. It is simplified through exclusion of the impertinent, and yet is intensified and given dramatic energy through the presentation of well directed contrasts and the ennoblement of all participating forms. The drapery will drape and render speaking, but neither overload nor obscure, the action of the figures; while the action of each will fit so perfectly into the action of the others, that no detail can be altered without disturbance of the whole.

In all these qualities the compositions of Raphael are approaching the noblest manner of antique sculpture, but without direct or conscious imitation.[22] His painting, and with greater emphasis, the sculpture and painting of Michelangelo, are rising to the level of the work of Scopas or Praxiteles, even to that of the masters of the Parthenon. The great art of Raphael and Michelangelo ascends to the peak of excellence reached by the ancient masters, not necessarily by following in their footsteps, but by climbing, it may be, the opposite side of the mountain.

Of a surety Italian painting had never been ignorant of the antique, had never been slow to borrow whatever figures or patterns or ideas it felt impelled to use; sometimes it would appear mindful of the antique lessons, and again quite disregardful of them. Whatever detail might be borrowed, the painting of Ghirlandajo, in general motive, form, and composition, was as unantique as possible. With the same antique background behind them, Raphael and Michelangelo in the clear development and progress of their Italian arts of painting and sculpture approach the classical. They have adopted, and made vitally their own, principles of composition, conceptions of beauty, realistic idealizing methods of compassing artistic excellence, all intimately related to the ways of ancient sculptors. But if, for instance, Michelangelo had any direct forbear, it was Signorelli and no antique statue; and, passing over the disputes as to details of his early instruction,

22 Of course, Raphael borrowed scores of antique decorative patterns, frankly enough: as one may see abundantly in the Loggia of the Vatican. And sometimes he manifestly imitates the ancient sculpture, as in the nude figure of Apollo (?) in the niche to the left of the centre in the *School of Athens*. But in the grand manner of his composition there would seem to have been no conscious copying of the antique. Doubtless he had drawn the symmetry of his compositions from Perugino or Fra Bartolommeo, even as for energy in action he drew upon Michelangelo and Leonardo.

we know that Raphael first imitated Perugino, then availed himself of what he could learn from Florentine painting, and took his last lessons from Michelangelo.

It was through mastering all these lessons, and the vital absorption into his own artistic faculty of the influences composing his physical and spiritual environment, that Raphael, prince of painters, brought to expression the last possibilities of his genius—of himself; the last possibilities which he might realize before dying at the age of thirty-seven in the year 1520, to the grief of Italy.

We have nothing of Raphael that reveals him except his painting. There we stop. Leonardo and Michelangelo have left much besides,—Leonardo some thousands of pages of manuscript which disclose the workings of his mind. Besides Michelangelo's poems, there are hundreds of his letters, many to his father and brothers disclosing his devoted and querulous affection, and his habit of living miserably and complaining of it. He writes to his father from Rome in 1512: "I live in a miserable fashion, caring neither for life nor for honors . . . and I suffer excessive hardships assailed by a thousand anxieties. It is now about fifteen years since I had an hour's repose, and all that I have ever done has been to help you; and you have never . . . believed it. God pardon us all." [23]

To his brother Buonarroti: "I live here surrounded by the greatest anxieties, suffering the greatest bodily fatigues. I have not a friend of any sort, and I do not want one; I have not so much time as suffices for me to eat the necessary food. However, I trust I may have no additional worries, for I could not bear another ounce." [24]

Michelangelo did live miserably at Rome and elsewhere. While working on Pope Julius's statute at Bologna, he did not take off his clothes or boots for weeks at a time, and slept in the same bed with his three workmen. On removing his boots the skin might peel off with them. His

[23] Trans. from R. W. Carden, *Michelangelo, a Record of his life as told by his letters*, p. 84.
[24] Ib. p. 63, Rome 1509.

letters show how wretchedly he kept himself, complaining always. He was difficult and violent in temper, suspicious, thinking that people were cheating him. He was nervous and timid. When about twenty, he cleared out of Florence with a man who had had bad dreams of the coming downfall of Piero dei Medici.[25] Thirty-five years later, while directing the fortifications of his city during the fatal siege, he fled again, suddenly, to Venice; a letter of his tells about it.[26] He could also be very prudent politically, avoiding speech with the Florentine exiles at Rome, lest it compromise him.[27]

Such apparent weakness of character may be only indirectly relevant. But the man's virtues were touched with weakness, at least with lack of judgment. Michelangelo was generous, the main support of a father as complaining as himself; he was always helping his brothers and a nephew whom he eventually made his heir, and wrote quantities of letters to, the following among them: "As I was quite unable to decipher thy last letter, I put it in the fire." [28] He was comically obstructive touching this nephew's marriage, objected, for example, to a wife who was near-sighted; altogether he was fearful of the ways of women. Besides his family, Michelangelo was generous and affectionate toward Urbino, his trusted servant. He would show impulsive love for those he liked, whether or not they were worthy of his regard. His praise was apt to be as extreme as his anger or irritation. He could debase himself before mediocrity, and was over-grateful to Vasari, who, of course, worshipped him. Yet he can write with very noble modesty, as to one Martelli who had sent him a sonnet in his praise: "I perceive that you have imagined me to be as God wished me to be. I am a simple man and of

---

25 Condivi, *Life of Michelangelo Buonarroti,* § XIV. This *Vita* speaks from a close intimacy with Michelangelo, and was published some years before he died.

26 Carden, o. c. p. 168 (Letter dated Sept. 25, 1529).

27 See letter of March, 1548, o. c. p. 232.

28 Carden, o. c. p. 248 (1548).

little worth, spending my time in striving to give expression to the art God gave me." [29]

Michelangelo had deep affection for Sebastian del Piombo, and praised him prodigiously,[30] as well he might; but he ascribed Raphael's success to his great diligence. The passionate devotion expressed for Tommaso Cavalieri, a cultivated Roman gentleman of great personal beauty, falls in the same category with the love for Victoria Colonna, soon to be referred to in connection with the sonnets.

The mention of these paltry incidents of character is pardonable if they prove not quite irrelevant to the self-expression of this complete and prodigious artist personality. Michelangelo adored beauty, and, above all, the beauty which might be rendered through the human form, which he glorifies in his painting and sculpture as Pindar glorified it in his Odes. Not altogether painter, but altogether artist, he seems to us. His temperament, his impulses and devotion, his imagination, his intellect and faculty, the complete efficient nature of the man, drew the whole compass of his life,—knowledge, opportunity, experience and incidental passion,—into the creation of beauty through the media of poetry, sculpture, painting, and architecture. He was an artist, and he lived no other life, save casually, distractedly, impertinently, under the passing jar of insignificant irritations, fears, and small infatuations.

With soft human spots in his soul, he might be hungry for affection, or, rather, might feel the need of feeling affection and expressing it. He cast his pearls before objects worthy or unworthy. His need was to cast his pearl, but not that the pearl should be taken into some warm and sympathetic bosom. Such an artist's love is like the first love of a youth, whose need is to love, and feel and think it out to its full reaches, imagine its relations with the eternal stars, express it in hidden or fearfully revealed

29 Carden, o. c. p. 185 (Jan'y, 1542).
30 Carden, o. c. p. 154, letter of May, 1525.

adoration. This love is most fortunate when not returned. For responsive affection from the object of it would check the youth's imagination, and might clog the expansion of his nature and faculties.

So with the love of an artist, an artist in his whole nature and through all his years, like Michelangelo. The youthful lover is or should be a poet. This artist was always young, loving imaginatively, seeking to clothe his affection in beauty. Michelangelo's love, as we find it in his poems, was Petrarchian, expressional and creative. It was the artist's love for the thing of beauty which he creates, while likewise uplifting to the spheres his conception of devotion to it. Unwise Pygmalion, to wish to have his statue come to life, in response to the love which had created it! The love expressed in Michelangelo's sonnets looked for no more return than did the ardor which he put into his painting and his sculpture. An equivalent return from the object of these impassioned expressions would have perplexed him; he could not have recognized himself as a fitting altar for such worship. He might even have been in a predicament; as if those creatures of his brush upon the Sistine ceiling, or, horror upon horror, those in the Last Judgment, had come to life and were thronging to clasp the knees of their creator and cover him with their Titanic affection!

We may not err in finding the sonnets of Michelangelo and the passionately sublime thought contained in them, to be sheer art. In them thought and imagination and emotion fuse and press with energy to artistic utterance; while the upper reaches of human passion are forced along the tortuosities of a hyper-poetic imagination. Were the sonnets an expression of a real passion? Assuredly; but it was a passion for beauty, perhaps rather for the expression or the creation of beauty; and not for the possession of the body and soul of another human being. They were the self-expression of the poet who composed them, and incidentally accepted the suggestions of certain actual relationships or experiences. The suggestions sprang from actuality; and the sonnets in which they were uplifted and finally enshrined were as true as art could make them. Theirs was the truth of valid and beautiful conceptions set in fitting words.

As befitted a sixteenth century Italian, this artist was less great as poet than as painter and sculptor. He seems to have composed verses through most of his life, certainly throughout the latter portion of it. He did not fling them off casually and carelessly; but corrected and rewrote them, and permitted a collection of them to be made for circulation among chosen spirits who could understand. The latest editor of these difficult poems [31] believes that he has succeeded in printing them in their proper temporal sequence; though often he has felt less certain of the individuals to whom they were sent, or addressed in the poet's mind. A number were addressed to a man, Cavalieri, [32] and these gave rise to the same questionings which have attached to some of Shakespeare's sonnets. In both cases the answers lie in the poet's impulse to express himself, already commented on. A more interesting analogy may be found in the way each of these poets has used the literary conventions in the air about him, and made of them vehicles for his own powerful and significant self-expression.

From the affinities of his own nature, Michelangelo revered Dante and felt the power of Dante's meaning. Occasionally he uses the metre of the *Commedia,* and his verse becomes Dantesque in phrase. But Petrarch afforded the chief store of conventional conceits and images. Michelangelo's thought also reflects the current Platonism of the Medici circles, as well as the sinuous far off rivulets of seeming Platonism which had percolated through Italian

[31] *Die Dichtungen des Michelagniolo Buonarroti,* herausgegeben etc., by Carl Frey (Berlin 1897). The first critical edition, that of C. Guasti, (Florence 1863), contains helpful prose renderings of the contents of each poem. J. A. Symonds's translations of the Sonnets must suffice for the English reader. They are not always the equivalent of the Italian; but represent a brave attempt at the impossible.

[32] E.g. Sonnet 50 (Frey's edition), beginning *Se nel volto.*

lyrics. Whether he read Plato for himself has been much disputed.

A number of these sonnets and madrigals are Petrarchian in sentiment and phrase. The query, for example, whether the beauty seen by the lover in his mistress is verily in her or in his own soul, is an echo of Petrarch as well as Dante.[33] But all such apparently borrowed notes have been revitalized in Michelangelo's deeply emotional as well as deeply intellectual nature, and reemerge in the sonnets as elements of his own rending self-expression.

Power, rather than facility, marks the work of Michelangelo, whether in marble or pigment or in verse. There is neither ease nor clarity in his sonnets. One feels in them first the difficulty of the thought, and then the power which compels the words to do the master's utterance. No other sonnets, Italian, French or English, evince such strainings. Yet the mind breaks through and conquers. And, when love is the burden of the sonnet, though the lines may not keep their significance sweetly and surely human, love is the more sublimely lifted to its eternal goal of beauty; and the love of beauty in mortal form unites with the love of the beauty and goodness of God.

Some of the sonnets move with the feeling of an individual or reciprocal situation. Surely those do which express the grieving thought of Michelangelo on the death of Victoria Colonna. But still he is an artist and a poet, obeying the compulsions of his conception of eternal love and beauty. The personal feeling or situation of the writer seems to inspire and guide the poems giving utterance to sorrow and contrition over the caducity and vain waste of life, when at the end the soul must cast itself on the piteous saving sacrifice of Christ. Alas! when it knows itself near death, but far from God!—

presso a morte e si lontan da Dio.[34]

Michelangelo wrote a number of sonnets and fragments

[33] No. 32 (Frey)—Dimmi di gratia. See Frey's notes.
[34] No. 48 (Frey), and see 49.

of sonnets having this theme in the last years of his life, and among them the most famous of all his poems:

Giunto è gia'l corso della vita mia. . . .[35]

Now that his life has reached the port where account of every unhappy or good deed must be given, alas for the life-long passion, the *affectuosa fantasia,* which has made art for him *idol' e monarcha!* Death is near and certain, and the second death, the everlasting, menaces. Neither painting nor carving can calm the soul now turned to that love divine which to receive us opens his arms upon the cross.

If the poems of Michelangelo were to be for the world the least important exponent of his genius, they illuminate the passionate tension of his sculpture and his painting. Also they show the manifold completeness of this man of four natures, as he was called, or of four gifts or faculties, which unfolded themselves in his four arts of poetry, sculpture, painting and architecture. These four arts were the expressions of his nature which was one in its manifold striving to create the beauty which it yearned to realize. The poems gave their harnessed utterance to the same endeavor which the mightier plastic genius of the man was embodying in sculpture and painting. St. Peter's dome was its last realization. Through all his arts, though in architecture least articulately, he sought to express the forms of visible beauty. Its highest type was the human form, the veritable human body stripped of obscuring accessories and distractions.

The instincts of his dynamic nature turned to the masculine rather than the feminine form; and in the masculine achieved its grandest triumphs: the *Adam* of the Sistine ceiling is incomparably more beautiful than the *Eve*: though one may stand astounded before the feminine figure of *Night* in the Medici Chapel. But the sheer decorative idealized athletic figures on the painted beams of the Sistine ceiling are all male. No man before or since ever drew

[35] No. 147 (Frey).

forth such import and beauty from the trunk and limbs of man. Yet when the figure and situation warranted, he gave proportionate emphasis to the human visage, as the crowning and most complex and subtle feature of the human form.

None had ever shown such knowledge of the human form; and no man's work approached such miracles of expressive tension and repose. Michelangelo studied and followed nature, the natural body; and then along the principles of its organic structure he passed beyond his source, surpassed his teacher. He is the grand exponent of Leonardo's pregnant words, the artist disputes and vies with nature, that his work may present further beauties and perfections through following the principles and suggestions of the natural world.

The work of no other artist has ever represented such enormous effort; and one may doubt whether the work of any other artist has surpassed it in achievement. The vocabularies of critics have been drained bare in describing these stupendous creations of sculpture and painting, or in criticising their alleged exaggerations and possibly baneful effect upon the following time. The effect may be condoned for the sake of the achievement! There is no call here to go beyond the works themselves or add to the discussion of them. The *Pietà*, the Sistine Ceiling, those recumbent demi-gods of pain on the Medici tombs, the statues in the niches over them, the Slaves in the Louvre, the *Moses* in S. Pietro in Vincoli, are exhaustless in beauty and import. They are like the Bible, like Shakespeare, like the Phidian Parthenon or the Cathedral of Chartres. Each thoughtful person shall appreciate and draw from them according to his understanding; and a residue will still be there! They were the self-expression of a daemonic artist.

It seems absurd to end this chapter without any reference to Venetian painting, which was so utterly expressive of the whole esthetic soul of Venice. The Venetian soul cast itself upon painting and color. Painting, colored decoration, was their art, their art *par excellence,* almost their sole and single art. Was this due to their affinity with the Byzantine East, where art was color rather than salient modelling? Was it due to their own atmosphere and sea and sunset? Who knows? The fact remained: Venice was all for painting. Her sculpture was insignificant, her poetry a blank.

But the field becomes too vast. Venetian painting is better to look at, and surrender one's self to, than to read and write about. All painting is primarily to be seen; but Venetian painting is somewhat more altogether to be seen rather than reflected on. Is not this true of Titian? He loved the naked body quite as dearly as did Michelangelo, and painted its flesh, its feminine color far more exquisitely. But Michelangelo's bodies, not Titian's, are meet for thought and reflection. The glories of the Venetian master's color surpassed all the coloring of Florence and of Rome; while the blander harmonies of his composition equalled Raphael's achievement. And he was a grand inaugurator of landscape painting.

And what like things might be said of *his* master Giorgione? And of Veronese? And what more like things, and other things besides, of that last Venetian Titan of a painter, Tintoretto, who seems to hurl his compositions on the canvas, miracles of light and dark. Nevertheless, there is too much to write about, or it is all better to be seen.